# New Poetries IV

ELEANOR CRAWFORTH was born in Manchester in 1982 and read English Literature at Fitzwilliam College, Cambridge. She joined Carcanet Press in February 2005, where she works in Sales and Marketing. She edits the 'News & Notes' section of *PN Review* and reviews for the magazine. She is studying for an MA in Post-1900 Literatures, Theories and Cultures at the University of Manchester.

STEPHEN PROCTER was born in London in 1981 and studied Philosophy at University College London followed by an MA in Renaissance and Romantic Literature at the University of Liverpool. He joined Carcanet in October 2004, where he works in Sales and Marketing. He is studying for a PhD at the University of Liverpool and is a book reviewer.

MICHAEL SCHMIDT OBE FRSL is Professor of Poetry at the University of Glasgow, and a poet, novelist and translator. He is the author of the critical history *Lives of the Poets* (1999), *The Story of Poetry* (five volumes, 2001-), and *The First Poets: Lives of the Ancient Greek Poets*. He edited *The Harvill Book of Twentieth Century Poetry in English* (2000) and Malcolm Lowry's *Under the Volcano* (Penguin). Michael Schmidt is Editorial and Managing Director of Carcanet Press and editor of the journal *PN Review*.

Also available from Carcanet Press

# New Poetries IV

*Edited by*
Eleanor Crawforth, Stephen Procter
and Michael Schmidt

CARCANET

First published in Great Britain in 2007 by
Carcanet Press Limited
Alliance House
Cross Street
Manchester M2 7AQ

Introduction copyright © Eleanor Crawforth and Stephen Procter 2007
Selection copyright © Eleanor Crawforth, Stephen Procter and
Michael Schmidt 2007

A CIP catalogue record for this book is available from the British Library
ISBN 978 1 85754 897 6

The publisher acknowledges financial assistance from Arts Council England

Typeset by XL Publishing Services, Tiverton
Printed and bound in England by SRP Ltd, Exeter

# Contents

# Introduction

When, from time to time, journalists inquire into 'the state of British poetry', they round up the usual suspects, gather sound-bites, lament that nothing quite measures up to the work of the luminaries of the recent past (Hughes, Larkin, Gunn), mention as if they were a coherent avant-garde the Cambridge 'experimental' school (now so well-established as to seem historical), and identify a couple of names as fingerposts to the future.

Yet the term 'British poetry' has morphed in recent years. If we use the term 'British' seriously in discussing poetry today, what do we mean? 'American poetry' has at least a geographical definition, however various the work of that continent is; even expressions such as the 'American line' and an 'American diction' suggest something almost specific. By contrast, the poetries of the British Isles divide out into national categories (Welsh, Scottish, Northern Irish) and into the English regions (London, the Midlands, the North and so on), but they are rarely characterised as *English* per se. Often the geographical identifier is abandoned early on and other categories – political, ethnic, theoretical, gender-based, or aesthetic – are invoked.

The evolving tradition of British poetry thrives, however. It is inclusive, incorporating formal and thematic lessons learned from other Anglophone and foreign poetries. One reason we can be deceived into regarding our poetry as impoverished is that many new writers do not aspire to write in a traditionally British way. That they do not is among the sources of strength in their poetry: they know where they come from and they want to move on in a spirit not of rejection but of extension.

This book is not primarily an anthology of British poetry. Though most of the poets included live or have lived in Britain, four do not travel on British passports. We do not attempt here to map cross-cultural trajectories. It would be limiting and counter-productive, we feel, to produce an anthology focused by the accidents of geography and politics. That we do not need the protection of isolation; that belonging implies – indeed entails – a blurring of borders, and a consequent enhancement of resources, is part of this new sense of Britishness. The anthology is published from Britain, edited by British editors: it provides a vista across a world-scape from a fixed point.

And it reflects the ways that some of the best emerging poetries are written by intellectually well-travelled and internationally curious individuals. Kei Miller contemplates this enriching uncertainty of poetic boundaries when he writes (in 'How we became the pirates', p. 63) that 'English poetry is no longer from England'. Cross-currents are felt repeatedly: a Caribbean poet reworks Shakespeare; a teacher in Suffolk discovers hailstones in Texas; a Scot takes his bearings from Latin American writers.

Christian Campbell, of The Bahamas and Trinidad and Tobago, engages with and moves outwards from the poetries of Kamau Brathwaite, Derek Walcott and Lorna Goodison. Like Kei Miller, from Jamaica, Campbell is suggestively at home in the spaces between the Caribbean, the United Kingdom and the United States. He celebrates full-throatedly, but also has the quiet precision to deliver anecdote and the laconic irony to place himself not only in but against the traditions he writes from. In 'Dover to Accra', a take on Matthew Arnold's 'Dover Beach', England's famous white cliffs are replaced by the luxurious beach villas of bourgeois Barbados. Campbell takes an iconic nineteenth-century British poem and runs with it in a different direction: 'I am running this morning to Dover Beach, fighting / to ignore Matthew Arnold, who is going someplace where / "the cliffs of England stand".' This persistent, reassuring emblem of English identity is affectionately displaced by the sound of American hip hop at a beach party, reflecting a contemporary Caribbean culture which is fluid, permeable and, as Campbell demonstrates, more multifarious than the familiar 'Little England, Little Africa' approach that has not quite had its day on either side of the Atlantic.

Andrew Frolish's poems lyrically evoke vast, open landscapes, both geographical and imaginative. Shifting from the plains of Texas to those of East Anglia, his poems are populated by memory and loss, of a father ('Construction' and 'Deconstruction') and of a beloved home ('Lavender Moon'). The man-made gathers emotional significance as natural and synthetic spaces collide; elegies are built around and contained within physical structures. Frolish's loose, flowing stanzas remain conscious of origin and personal history.

A psychologist by profession, Beatrice Garland writes poems which return to images of childhood, family and memory. Encountering refugees, gypsies and even a reptilian species on the verge of extinction, her sympathies lie with the homeless, nomadic and displaced. She confronts the mute terror of female war victims ('A Kosovan ghost story') and the prehistory of the earth ('The end of the pterodactyls'), juxtaposing violence and beauty to startling effect. Highly visual, her poems engage the senses: in the filmic 'Crow Aptok', for example, images of suburban England accelerate past the window of a train, revealing a secret life of butterflies, birds and trainspotters. There are poems, too, of tactile sensuality; in 'Parts of Speech', she imagines a grammatology of love.

Emma Jones, the Australian writer, creates carefully shaped poems that are light and precise. Danger and energy tense and unsettle her tightly crafted lines. In her vividly electric poem 'The Tiger in the Menagerie', for example, suspense builds gradually beneath the taut calm of her prosody:

If the menagerie could, if would say 'tiger'.

If the aviary could, it would lock its door.
Its heart began to beat in rows of rising birds
when the tiger came inside to wait.

In her world, the inanimate comes alive (cages, bars, pearls, mirrors, coins, the moon), the elemental is anthropomorphised (the sea, trees, wind, the seasons, song). Haunting and multi-layered, permeated by the 'inner algorithms' of the natural world, her poems linger in the ear and on the tongue.

Gerry McGrath discovered his vocation for poetry on a journey from Glasgow to Crianlarich on a Scottish summer's day. The poems remain preoccupied with journeys, real or imagined. He is a passionate reader whose writing has been shaped by European influences, among them Russian, Czech, Polish; but his poems typically move across sparsely populated, unmistakably Scottish landscapes. The short, haunting lyrics risk abstraction and deliberately fragment prosodic patterns to bring alive transient moments and images: a seascape ('The Colour of Water'), the gravitational pull on waves ('Element'), the beginning of a morning train journey to an unknown city ('Anstruther'). The everyday connects naturally with the universal, personal journeys and stories merge with elemental cycles. 'We see things / you and I...the skin of a pool / a lighthouse beam / of frost.'

Kei Miller, who writes fiction as well as verse and whose poems often begin in story-telling, has learned much from American and

British poets, and much also from his landscapes and the language of his native Jamaica. He – like Campbell – explores the at once alienating and liberating state of being 'in-between' – Jamaica and England, belonging and not belonging. His elegies emerge in the vivid colours and dancehall rhythms of his part of the Caribbean; mothers, aunts, sisters, daughters and the 'church women' of middle-class Jamaican society have a place in his poems. Moving from Peckham, South London to Kingston, Jamaica by way of Manchester and Mumbai, he makes human connections in a world of displacements. His powerful sequence of love poems, 'The Broken', maps the topography of human relationships:

Borders are jagged; every island is proof…
Love is how our skin breaks against each other,
how we bleed into each other, and how
we heal.

Christopher Nield's raw, uneasy poems can deliver new ways of seeing. He experiments with rhyme and metre to striking effect; he can deploy a pantoum, a terzanelle or a sonnet; indeed, for him form is the beginning of statement. From the ekphrastic 'Two Cardinals Painted by El Greco' to the sexually charged 'Aphrodite', a twenty-first-century ode to classical beauty, and 'Sancreed', a meditation on spiritual superstition, Nield's poems use with great freshness the languages of religious iconography and the visual arts. A fairy tale of ambiguous gender politics ('Kay's Song') appears alongside a villanelle about love and loss on the London Underground ('The Difference You Make') and a playful celebration of a lover's paunch ('What It's Like, After All'). He is not shy of approaching the morbid or uncomfortable with dark humour. Around the real there is always the hint of a fantastical lining.

Born in Sydney, Australia, and now living in New Zealand, Joanna Preston moved between various Australian towns during her childhood. The one constant feature in this nomadic existence was her grandparents' farm in Cowarral, not far from Les Murray's in Bunyah. The ecological awareness of Preston's fellow Antipodean had a formative influence upon her work. Murray's concern for the changing environment of the Australian outback, and the earthiness of Ted Hughes both affected her. Her poems evoke an integrated and organic world threatened by destruction, both human and natural (as in 'Parable of the Drought'). Preston's enigmatic, direct lyrics find beauty in ordinary objects – an empty house, a 'bloodied feather', her grandmother's gloves.

An admirer of the American tradition of Stevens, Frost and Moore, Edward Ragg strives to arrest vital 'spots of time' in a language which is tightly formal and crafted; fleeting moments of vision are 'sealed and meant'. His 'Narco Poem', for instance, portrays how elusive and suggestive language can be, the poem conducted by a fraught, restless and insomniac speaker. His exacting gaze and his engagement with the outer limits of phenomenology owe something to Stevens. Poetry becomes a form of imaginative travel, a broadening out of horizons. His monologue 'The Parochial Man' encourages us to read outside our own immediate sphere of experience: its hero seeks out 'other parishes...beyond the name of any town / Or part of sea, or lighthouse, bunker, cave...' Disclosing the global within the local and vice versa, the poem sets out 'To see how the villages look from up / Above: the native fields, the flowers in them.' Ragg has recently moved to China, a further world in which his nets of language will snare memorable image and sense.

Like Christopher Nield, Philip Rush has an instinct for the magical and 'unreal'. With freedom of association, he moves with the reader into unfamiliar yet credible landscapes in which we encounter the mystical nomadic tribes of the Sahara ('Tuareg'), the 'sea-fog' of 'the Galician, the Asturian shore' ('Percebes') and the sinister traditions of a fairy tale village ('Custom'). Uncontained by rigid structures, Rush's poems answer to the disciplines of a pure imagination, evoking 'kinds of sorcery' which free us from mere contingency. For him, poetry is a generative and re-generative process which tests unarticulated beliefs, challenges prejudices, extends knowledge: 'The language stands out to be counted.'

As a young, gay, London-born Asian poet, Saradha Soobrayen explores the possibilities of versification and poetics through a series of poems that risk the big themes of love and loss. Unsettling encounters find tender resolutions through a playful and assured use of formal and free verse. Lovers continually just miss one another, moving on parallel planes, failing to connect ('From the writing room'). When they finally do meet, it is with exhilarating velocity. Her verse is fed from many sources, and the variety of diction, rhythm and form is remarkable, from the Mauritian Creole of 'Mo Ti Bébé' to the epic 'My Conqueror', a dramatic monologue that confronts slavery and imperialism, envisaging a romantic encounter between a *conquering* female Napoleon and a *conquered* female island.

Soobrayen's poems combine radical post-colonial and gender politics with sensual enchantment; her exuberant imagery and delicate forms and rhythms complement one another in unusual ways.

There are more points of contrast than of convergence between the eleven poets included here. Gerry McGrath and Christopher Nield may both experiment with lineation in short, condensed stanzas; Beatrice Garland and Saradha Soobrayen may make poetry from the components of speech; Andrew Frolish and Joanna Preston may develop an ecological consciousness by means of nature poetry. Such affinities do not constitute affiliation: as with earlier *New Poetries*, the irreducible plural of the title remains key. Yet all eleven are fascinated by form and the paradoxical liberation that constraint affords; by the diversity of languages available, and by what the present world and the present tense have to offer.

Eleanor Crawforth
Stephen Procter

# Christian Campbell

CHRISTIAN CAMPBELL, of The Bahamas and Trinidad and Tobago, was born in Freeport, Grand Bahama, on June 22, 1979. A poet, cultural critic and journalist, he resides in Nassau, the Bahamas. He read English at Balliol College, University of Oxford as the 2002 Commonwealth Caribbean Rhodes Scholar and completed a PhD at Duke University.

He has presented and published his work widely in magazines and anthologies in the Caribbean, the United States, Britain and Switzerland. A Cave Canem Poetry Fellow and Arvon Foundation graduate, he was a member of the Bahamian National Swim Team. His manuscript, 'Running the Dusk', was named runner-up finalist for the 2005 Cave Canem Poetry Prize by Sonia Sanchez.

# Dover to Accra

*for Kamau Brathwaite*

I go running from my woman's house in Dover
Gardens to Dover Beach in order to keep my body
tight for her, as well as to reason with my insides,
and take her route on the road – *left, right, left, then follow
the curve down to the beach (keep South)*. This area
is bourgeois Barbados with houses that are not extravagant
but comfortable in their gorgeousness – crowds
of bougainvillea, croton, hibiscus, pastel houses with Spanish
roofs, hurricane shutters, large terracotta vases. I want
a house here in Dover, I think as I run, and suddenly
petit bourgeoisie turns to tourism. A quaint Italian restaurant,
two German women in bathsuits and flip-flops on the people's road,
a taxi driver posted on the corner outside of the Casuarina
Beach Club like a sentinel, at attention under his flags:
Broken Trident, Union Jack, Stars and Stripes. Any minute now
I expect to see a man with rusty dreadlocks, and I turn
the curve into stands of shell and coconut souvenirs.

I am running this morning to Dover Beach, fighting
to ignore Matthew Arnold, who is going someplace where
'the cliffs of England stand'. But before I know it,
Arnold gets bust in the chops, his bushy mutton chops,
by Sean Paul: *BREAKOUT BREAKOUT (bruk wine),
BREAKOUT BREAKOUT!* At last my dreadlocked spar
toting a boombox on his shoulder, more and more
whitepeople and Dover Beach is there. Running Dover
twice through, I meet an obstacle course of umbrellas, palms
and lounge chairs cradling people as red and wrinkled
as salt prunes; they are English so they want to sunbathe
and then see their ruins. Up the surf are a few braiders and rent-
a-dreads but Bajans don't quite hustle and shuffle like us. Dover
Beach is a smallish stretch of sand prostrating before jubilant blue.

I am here in Dover, in Christchurch, Barbados, with my woman
who is beautiful and waiting for me, who has always waited for me.
And when I return from my run, we will spend the day at Accra
Beach. Kamau Brathwaite, Bajan poet, said,

---

'Barbados, most English of West Indian islands,
but at the same time nearest, as the slaves fly, to Africa.'
We will go from Dover to Accra with my woman's friends,
two generations of *bounda Ma Jacques* pretty Dominican women
and I will tell them all that their beaches are nothing compared
to my pink coral sand and water like blue chiffon in The Bahamas,
*baja mar*, shallow sea. I will go the colour of molasses mixed
with bronze, the tone of a sweet, dark rum in Accra,
and we will all swallow the sun whole on Accra
Beach, near the hotel, in Little England, Little Africa,
in love with skin on this second day of the year.


## At Buckingham Palace

### I

I am the first of my family
to go to Buckingham Palace.
I had the flu, I nearly stayed home.
Left my hair in all its might,
wore a beige linen suit.

Her Majesty was in a red dress
with horrid black elbow gloves,
her hair like rigor mortis.
She was very, very calm.

Van Dyck, Rubens,
Rembrandt, Canaletto
from all angles, oil paintings
on the ceilings and walls. The eyes
of Anglo nobles glaring down,
draperies, mirrors and all.

Sèvres porcelain, Canova
and Chantrey sculpture,
servants, secret rooms,
French furniture.
But no crown jewels
from India in sight,
none from Benin.

*Mister, Mister,*
*where have you been?*
*I been to London*
*to see the Queen.*

Some of the ladies curtsied,
some of the men bowed.
The Queen raised her black glove
high and looked away, too posh
to be stared in the eye.
But I wish she heard Tosh
chanting out my mind:
*Light your chalice,*
*Make we smoke it inna*
*Buk In Hamm Palace.*

## II

The Queen came to Nassau
on a royal visit when I was eight.
The whole family walked
out to streets lined like Boxing Day,
to see her pass in a green Jaguar,
to see that white-gloved wave
borrowed in pageants, float parades.

Benjamin Zephaniah, Rasta poet,
turned down the OBE. *Up yours,*
he said, *No way Mr Blair, no way Mrs Queen.*
When my grandfather got that MBE,
name blazing on the Queen's
New Year's Honours List,

Her Majesty told him something
that he would stage for guests
for years, displaying his medal
as a child shows a good wound.
*Wear your best suit,* he would have said,
*Make sure cut your hair, shine up*
*your shoes.*

## Briland Aubade

*for Lorna Goodison*

Chanticleers flounce around
like Lord Dunmore must have done,
broad-chested and pompous,

brilliantly plumed. They have broken
their pact with the Briland sun.
Too aloof for a dayclean crow,

they let the island sleep in,
call out when they please.
Briland only big enough

for golf carts, to sput through
archways draped with bougainvillea,
red crown canopy

for a bride and groom, through
rock roads of cocoa plum bush,
sea grape, dark blushing croton.

Never pass an old woman
on her clapboard porch
without saying *Mornin.*

At the Pink Sands beach
we descend into peace breeze
and the sea rising like a staircase

of lapis lazuli, blues live
beyond belief. If Winslow Homer
painted this place, he'd paint

the small boys barking coconut
on the postcard shore
without eyes or mouths. But could he

catch the faint faint rose of the sand,
as if tinged by blood from a beach
massacre two hundred years ago?

Fish-belly models crane
and arch for a photoshoot
near pastel cottages.

Expats and winter residents lounge
in these twinned tropics
of Africa and New England,

in this wooden, white-fenced
commonwealth of skyjuice
and colonial slumber.

White Brilanders birthday their homes,
three hundred years of family
ground: Loyalists, Adventurers

from Bermuda, Preacher's Cavedwellers,
seekers of *Eleutheria*, Greek
for freedom, slavery,

apprenticeship, prohibition,
rum-running. Old Bahamian
prejudice. But the sea

forgives it all. Dunmore Town
hums with youths in psychedelic
Oakley shades, twine-up hair;

they run the rentals, prowl the docks
for prey as the young girls grow
ripe on Miami dreams.

What else is there to do
on an island big as a stone?
Drift like a tourist through

Colebrooke St and Dunmore St,
through *Eva's Straw Work* and *Dunmore
School, The Landing, Starfish Restaurant,*

*Nappy's* for the best gourmet pizza
and cracked conch, Ma Ruby's dinner
at *Tingum Village Hotel, Wesley Methodist*

*Church, Avery's* for a boil fish breakfast,
*Seagrapes Club, Vic-hum's Lounge,*
under the stars, best club on Briland.

Once you have touched
this Harbour Island, you are bound
to come back. We sing

*I got sand in my shoe,*
quadrille to rake 'n scrape
like the old people. Dunmore Town

is older than America
and we are two Nassau folks
seeking sea-song and romance.

At Romora Bay, I wake to silence,
to the sun's face pressed against
the mauve curtain, its morning veil.

I wake to you standing
naked in the mirror.
You are combing your hair.

## Cook

*Gyal yuh better can cook, tink yuh deya for yuh pretty looks*
*Yuh waan live ah restaurant and come dunn man bank book*
*Cook, eeh, recipe book*
*Gwaan inna di kitchen cause yuh hand dem nuh nook*

Lexxus, 'Cook'

I am frying my baby an omelette,
me one naked in front of the warm stove
wondering why good sex drives us to cook
things like sweat mixed with eggs (no yolk), onion,

pale cheese, tomato, green pepper, seasoned
well with salt, pepper, thyme and scotch bonnet
pepper sauce, seeping through thick egg stir-up
like lava. The pan will have been heating

on high all now to make large tears sizzle,
then lowered to let butter skate the pan
and bubble down into fluid, after
which the omelette can take shape and harden.

Heartstring comes, kisses my neck, nearly sings:
*I like scotch bonnet pepper on most things.*

# Rudical

*Derek Bennett, killed by the police*

*after Matisse's* Icare (Jazz), *1943*

I who born
Thirty-one years
Since *The Windrush* come
Thirty-one years
Life of a man
I who born
Forty-one bullets
Amadou Diallo
Life of a man
Seven kill me
I who born

     & because we suck the neon marrow of the streets
     & because we tote a solar plexus of islands (*it's true*)
     & because we yuck out the blue heart of night (*right*)
     & because our heads gather thick as a bloodclot (*teach them*)
     & because we eat out the honey of mad laughter (*everytime*)
     & because we outrun the delirium of streetlights (*OK*)
     & because we are gray bugs scuttling from the lifted rock
     & because & because & &
     & because high street skeets a thousand niggers
     & because my eyehole grows iridescent with the moon
     & because we holler for the bloodclad sun
     & because we mourn the burst testes of the stars
     & because we skank cross rivers of blood

Mine New Cross mine Oldham Notting Hill Bradford Brixton
mine too Nassau Laventille Bridgetown Kingston Britain has
branded an x in my flesh this rolled throat of killings this septic
eye this urge of maggotry this seed of Mars this blasted plot this
hurt hissing realm this ogly island this England

# Shells for Sonia Sanchez

You ten, I six, and jujube
now in season. I monkey up
the tree's weak bones and call
down to you, not Wilsonia, that
big-people name. I does call you
Nita. Only them small ocean eyes
that say how you know, I know,
my Mummy know that, boy, jujube
stain don't come out. I'll do most
anything for these plump little suns
and you, even with wasps telling
secret. Is breaktime still and your legs
look skinny under that plaid skirt. You is
give me quarters sometimes, to buy salty.
You's always have your hair in one,
rake and scrape to the side, and if
that don't mean womanish, I don't know
what does. You's the one that start everyone
saying, *That's my prerogative!* You stink
to them teachers but not one child at Xavier's
could test you at singing. I tell people
you's my cousin, but you really the one
that I lend my recorder to longtime
so you wouldn't get licks
and you did never forget it.

One time you tell me Santa Claus
fake cause we don't have no chimney
in Nassau and his skin too pink
for this kinda sun and I was sad
because I was hoping for one new bike
so you let me go first in handball. We always
have to pray every morning assembly
*Our father who art in heaven*
*Harold be thy name* and I ask you
why Harold so mean to never show
me his art? And the grin how you
answer is keep me glad for days.

I most tall as you, you know, but you
could beat me and plenty boys running
any day, quick as a curly-tail lizard.
Sometimes, when I feel like it, I go up
to people in the schoolyard and point
and say, *What you name?* and you laugh
big as America.

The children don't like me cause
I know my numbers and hard words too
and you say is cause they still is
pee the bed. The children say you
don't have no Mummy and your mouth
too hot. That mouth. Like two piece
of pepper, it stay poke out, a thing
shape for cussing. All neck and pointer
finger, tripping on your tongue. My
Miss Biggety, with your little red self.
Yes you. You who is hum for the trees
always and play ringplay and pinch
the boys that get too fresh. If I did know
you was going with your Daddy to leave
me for true, I would of give you all
my shells and soldier crabs, and even my
new chain. I would of make you learn me
to run fast and sing, if I did know New York
was far-far like the moon.

*and for Kerha*

# Curry Powder

*Panday in power now*, somebody cries.
*They think they better than people*,
my Trini cousins say, *And they like*
*wear Fila shoe*. My brother and I
laugh and add, *They is smell strong*
*like curry powder*. Is true, we insist.

Coolies and niggers fighting these days
but great-grandmummy Nita did not fight
when she found herself facing the West
instead, touching the Negro face of a Grenadian,
Manny. She did not wear saris no more.
Calypso she liked and could wind down
with the best of them. She became deaf
to the ethereal melody of *Krishna*'s flute.
She chose Manny, not *Lord Rama* in her
Hindu epic gone wrong. At her wedding
she never once uttered *Ganesh*'s name
and she loosened the grasp of *Vishnu*'s
four hands from round her waist.
So her sisters disowned her in the holy
name of Mother India. But she made
*dougla* babies anyway and did not give
them the sacred names of gods: *Brahma*,
*Shiva*, *Gauri*. She named Grandaddy
*Leon*, a good European name, like all the other
rootless Negroes. And so Trinidad became herself.

You know how people go, it took many deaths
and many births for the Mullchansinghs to talk
to the Brathwaites again and, finally, Mummy
and her siblings were born looking Indian enough.
But Panday in power now and Mummy warned
me to say *Indian* not *coolie*. One of my cousins
told me, with a grown-up intuition, *You know,*
*in Trinidad, you not black, you dougla.*

Panday in power now and my cousins still cuss
about neighbours with their jhandi flags of many colours
claiming their yards for as many gods as there are
colours. After enough cussing, we all go to eating
pelau with roti and curry, and so, with our fingers
stained yellow like old documents, we, too, stink
of curry powder.

# Andrew Frolish

ANDREW FROLISH was born in Sheffield in 1975. He studied politics at Lancaster University before training to be a primary school teacher in Ambleside in the Lake District. Since qualifying as a teacher, Frolish has lived with his wife in Suffolk, where he is a deputy head teacher. In 2007 Frolish celebrated the birth of his first child. His poems have been published in several magazines, including *Acumen, Envoi, Tears in the Fence, Pulsar, The Interpreter's House* and *PN Review*. In 2006, he won the Suffolk Poetry Society Crabbe Memorial Prize.

'Breathing' was first published in *The Interpreter's House*; 'The Pan of Rice Lady' was first published in *Envoi*, and 'Hailstones in Texas' and 'Return to Bird Rock' have been accepted for publication in *PN Review*.

# Hailstones in Texas

I mean this literally: the sky was green.
Green like the moss creeping its way through our lawn,
like the algae in the shallow pond by the back door.
Not the green of freshly mown grass,
but something darker and more substantial than that.

When we arrived at the ranch,
the dogs were deranged and howling,
running between the pellets of rain water,
dancing out of harm's way
and shaking vigorously when they failed.
Overhead, the porch light swung
from side to side, throwing our shadows
this way and that.

We howled and danced our way to the veranda,
soaked and raining like human clouds.
Someone made a fire while our socks clung to radiators
and we watched the storm through the open door:
leaves tossed about between bobbing trees;
garden furniture bounced against the workshop;
power lines swayed like drunks.

The rain turned to hail.
A sudden brightening layered the sky –
from a churning sea to the depths of her eyes.
And in that instant, the storm tossed a hailstone
the size of a man's fist across the veranda
and into the house.
It bounced to a stop beside the fire
and waited for the lazy warmth of the coals
to worry the edges of its coat of ice.
But one of us scooped it up
and laughed and hurled it outside.

That night the bolted door
was almost shaken off its hinges,
but it stood its ground and kept us in

as the stones drummed it like fingers.
And we danced in the dining room,
holding our partners close,
our footsteps drowning out
the punchy persistence of the hail.
Her cowboy boots slithered
over the polished floor,
a peel of new lizard skin
as the storm starved and thinned.


## Whalesong

We were listening for humpbacks:
the faint songs and callings
folded into the creases of the sea.
Breathing stalled; a pause in the bubbles
and froth of humanity misplaced,
lost and found in the wrong element,
light bending incorrectly in the translucence
beneath the shifting slick surface.

Then we dropped into the deepness
of swallowing blueness, breathing steadily,
accounting for changes in pressure
absently, automatically, the unthinking
reflexes of years not drowning
in places full of blue like this.

There's a magic in the act
of levitation above the sea bed,
rising and falling only with the drawing in
and exhalation of air from the aqualung,
skirting over the coral fans,
great purple bruises widening like sky.
Here the reef is reckless and rises
in steep walls and monuments
to the drifting of tides and time.

I miss the moray hidden in the fissure
and the nurse shark parked up
between the honeycomb
and the bloody crown-of-thorns.
Distracted by groupers and comical parrotfish,
I let the hawksbill pass through me
like a breeze through a ghost.

We rise, like heat, like souls,
and reach for the surface,
hands touching the glass window.
And we're sucking in real air
as if for the first time.
Before hauling our sodden bodies
up the ladder and onto the boat,
we pause, holding the life in our lungs,
heads lowered into the water
and listening again. Humpbacks.
They nod vigorously and laugh
and speak of nothing else for days.
My nodding hides the secret
of the silence. I lied. I failed.
I could never hear the whales.

# Breathing

The morning taste was acid
like dead skin and old paper,
like the stale attic
where I found the box years ago
(just yesterday).

As the light thinned out –
a time of fool's gold leaf –
the vodka flowed on
and the orange receded
until it was neat.

In those hours you came in and out
of the box, taken in and expelled
with my breathing.
Each breath I took
cloaked my throat with dust,
making it even harder to say
the words I avoided in the days
when I breathed easily.

# Lavender Moon

Many nights have flowed through the skies overhead,
dark, brooding floods of black cloud, leaving a stain
of sediment and memory on these walls and tiled peaks.
It is damp with it, soaked deep into the wattle and daub
and the oak floor bending and sagging under the weight of it.

I rest my hands on the beams, like veins
on these walls of pale skin, and I feel the life within,
the hum and throb of its heart, still strong
underneath its old skin, listen as it breathes in
and know that it has me like a drug.

These rooms inched in during the years we settled
like dust into the corners and crannies,
fingers shaping easily into fingers of wood and brick,
fist into palm, the house cupping us with love.
But these rooms are bare now and echo with the space we hid.

The scent of lavender from your secret garden
slips around the bedroom door, caressing me just once more
between the day before the last and the last
and I let it sweep over me and drink it in, warming my core.
With it, a silver silk of moon slides and touches my hand.

We lie together, waiting with the lavender moon
and sensing the flood overhead, unsaying our dream
that the moon will remember us ahead of all the others
and that your lavender will stray into this house
long after our passage through here is over.

# Construction

All the forces collide in him,
the electro-magnet, the compound heart,
the crucible of manufacturing.
In the blackened whorls of his fingers
are a thousand stains of invention,
blood spilled remains of oily assembly,
the carved metal of miners' lamps and stamps
of codes and places on his products –
the physical proof of his passing through.
In his hands, my father inspects the shining skin
of a new lamp, testing the spark as he forces the flint.

Beneath his overalls and grease and grime,
he is distinguished by a starched collar and tie.
Now see him, in this windowless place,
hand resting tenderly on a metal plate,
encouraging its hum, its tick, its work rate
with a carefully forged whisper, and they breathe
together, like one great machine, stronger
than the sum of my parts; they mould, make, measure.

In the artificial light, no one sees the cloud rise,
an invisible fog of chemical bile.
And yet he knows it; senses a shift in the atoms
and an interference in the cogs and whirs of creation.
This is a drama of working men. Evacuation.
While we make our way outside, blinded
by handfuls of summer light, he remains
to engineer a healing process, hands on.
Outside, I bask alone in the warmth of a summer
we had forgotten; formed in our absence.
My father follows the piston punching siren call
while workers wait in the shadow of the factory wall.

And this is how the myth of factory hero
is pieced together, a construction in time
of memorised tools, cogs, pumps and grime;
hands crafting over fists pummelling, a life
spent manufacturing this man; the myth is mine.

# Deconstruction

My father: naked without a tie,
his strength forged amongst
the obsolete machines and tools
of another forgotten time.

First they took his teeth,
wrenched from him
while he slept on white sheets.
Then they took his belief

and left him spitting blood
into screwed up tissues;
his shoulders bunched up,
reduced and subdued.

Bits of him were discarded
and replaced by wires and tubes,
LED displays and visiting rules.
Dripping bags tied him to the bed.

So finally the machines had him,
regulating his daily intake, his pain.
The tables were turned, turned innards out,
diminishing returns in a bandage of skin.

# Return to Bird Rock

The weather changed as we crossed the bridge at Barmouth,
leaving behind the light breeze that brushed our cheeks
like the breath of yesterday or the campfire wheeze at Dolgellau.
The sun grazed our necks: pale white to raw red to leather brown,
as our strength oozed from us in short gasps on the steeper slopes.
The silence between the fells, where the wind was stilled and
                                                choked
and the valleys were lines and wrinkles on green skin,
was filled by our graceless motion and our singing, unfazed
as we wanted to be by the miles before us, the hard days.

Convinced, as we were, that our gang was the first
to walk these ranging hills and cross these rivers,
we wrote our legend in our stories told long after.
And when the day slipped under and drowned
while we cowered by the canopies of secret trees,
it was just more meat on bones we have since picked clean.
Above it all rose Bird Rock, the crag time forgot,
bursting from the scorched earth like a lush, green marker,
a buoy, dancing on tides greater than we were.
I can picture it now, to the left, too far to walk to, too close
to ignore the tug of its gravity. But time short, we moved on.
Later, guiltily, we looked back. All the landmarks were gone.

Now look at us, you and me, the first to wilt and fold up neatly
into small cases in the boot of my car, looking for the place
in our hearts that we never felt ready to leave or exchange.
This time we have maps and patient directions as guides.
Still, the day is twisted out like a filament before we find it.
Bird Rock hunches over, disturbed, thinking we would never
                                                find it.
But though we climb it, and marvel at the white crystal drops of
                                                light
scattered on its back in downy flecks, there is a hole in our memory.
The view is right, along the creased valley to the far, grey sea;
and the map is right and we are right where we should be.
Bird Rock barely stirs as we mark our return.

---

# The Pan of Rice Lady

Her smouldering hair
sneaked up on us
like the pan of rice
that we seem to be in the habit
of boiling dry.

I smiled in disbelief
at the crazy woman
who cared so much
for her tin-pot cause
that she would burn.

Later, I reclined comfortably
and drank unsweetened tea,
thankful that nothing mattered
enough for me to die
in reckless passion.

# The Apple Peeler

The first attack is swift
between the raising of the glass
and the sip,
leaving a flap of skin
beneath the eye
bringing to mind
my grandma with a sharp knife
peeling an apple
within an inch of its life
maintaining the cut
all the way around;
spirals of green
falling away
like the blood on his shirt
easing into the fibres
in teardrop stains
allowing the surprise
to do the work.

Her control of the knife
taking none of the white
sliding under the skin
gliding over the bone
revealing the marrow
and bringing the blade
all the way home.

In the porcelain sink
where he washed away his face
there is a teaspoon of blood
instinctively touched
and I wipe it on the front of my jeans
where it will steal its way
into the fabric
putting down roots
and passing on the stain.

# Beatrice Garland

BEATRICE GARLAND was born in Oxford in 1938, and educated in a wide variety of institutions. After a degree in English Literature she went on to study the behaviour of rats, chimpanzees and later, human beings. She later became a Consultant Psychologist in the National Health Service, where she now works as a clinician, teacher and researcher. She developed a particular interest in the subject of trauma, working in England and abroad. She began to write poetry in 1989. Her work has been published in a number of magazines, including *PN Review*, the *London Magazine*, the *Spectator*, *The Rialto*, and in the anthology, *Poetry Introduction 8* (Faber, 1993). In 2001 she won the National Poetry Prize for 'Undressing' and in 2002 the Strokestown International Poetry Prize for 'Kamikaze'.

'Parts of speech', 'The end of the pterodactyls' and 'Undressing' appeared in the *London Magazine*; 'Kamikaze' has appeared in *PN Review*.

# Kamikaze

Her father embarked at sunrise
with a flask of water, a samurai sword
in the cockpit, a shaven head
full of powerful incantations
and enough fuel for a one-way
journey into history

but halfway there, she thought,
recounting it later to her children,
he must have looked far down
at the little fishing boats
strung out like bunting
on a green-blue translucent sea

and beneath them, arcing in swathes
like a huge flag waved first one way
then the other in a figure of eight,
the dark shoals of fishes
flashing silver as their bellies
swivelled towards the sun

and remembered how he
and his brothers waiting on the shore
built cairns of pearl-grey pebbles
to see whose withstood longest
the turbulent inrush of breakers
bringing their father's boat safe

– *yes, grandfather's boat* – safe
to the shore, salt-sodden, awash
with cloud-marked mackerel,
black crabs, feathery prawns,
the loose silver of whitebait and once
a tuna, the dark prince, muscular, dangerous.

*And though he came back*
*my mother never spoke again*
*in his presence, nor did she meet his eyes*
*and the neighbours too, they treated him*
*as though he no longer existed,*
*only we children still chattered and laughed*

*till gradually we too learned*
*to be silent, to live as though*
*he had never returned, that this*
*was no longer the father we loved.*
And sometimes, she said, he must have wondered
which had been the better way to die.

# Parts of speech

New languages begin like this.
At first, loose bits of alphabet
– an *S* reclining by an *X* –
lie randomly about the bed.

*L* for leg sprawls comfortably
across your body's upturned *Y*
and touch discovers difference,
exotic pronouns – *you*, and *I*.

Now knowledge stirs: curious, we add
the liquid vowels of intention,
using for our beginners' words
an *O*, an *aye*, to link and soften

syllables, the growing shapes
of joined-up speech. Next we find,
to understand the proper use
of mouth and hand, there's a need

for prepositions: *on* and *in*
and *over*, *under*, then *between*,
till the demand for the conjunction
from amateurs on fire to learn

exerts its fierce imperative –
and then our differences are gone:
we conjugate *to have, to be*,
joined so deeply we are one.

This is how I came to know
the fluent grammar of the face,
the body's lively, lucid text
– the tender writing of new verse.

# Crow Aptok

And look: crouched low and fast asleep,
house-backs, back yards, rear
extensions, washing lines, bedroom
windows with the curtains drawn,
black brick, parallel tracks – and
as the rocking train speeds by
each day new hieroglyphs,
the traces of gatherings, larks
while others were sleeping.
It's the artists again. They
do not own luggage or books.
They wear beanies of fleece
pulled down over their ears
and the gear slung low on their belts.
When the moonlit arc of the tracks
cuts a swathe through the city,
they are bats on the parapets,
gibbons on girders, cruisers
of cool steel, finding new cuttings,
bridges, embankments, the dark
noses of tunnels. And here
where the buddleias spark with
Cabbage White, Peacock,
Fritillary, they speak in tongues
and their legions are many:
*Rainman, Toxo, Slam, Fonz.*
The great *Crow Aptok*, the man
who could hood his eyes like a hawk.
(Once in the North was issued
his terrible final judgement:
*Landarse drools.*) Reputations
hang upon the bulge of their *a*s,
the rake of their proper nouns.
They are the night shift,
the artists of darkness.
*Remember me.*
*I was here. I was here.*

# The end of the pterodactyls

Imagine that irreversible pitch down:
one moment carried on a wind as loose
as silk, snakey with heat, they'd slip above
an emerald mat of forest draped in steam,
the shriek and skirmish of vermilion birds;
floating past lakes so clear they'd see
right down to where a slow escape of bubbles
rimmed in light would each raise up a dozen
grains of sand to glitter in the sun;
or watch the earthbound staring upwards, stilled
by their magnificent passage overhead –
until the icing-up of earth began.

And then the stuttering dive
through elements turned coldly alien,
an unsupporting air, a hostile wind
ripping the belly open stem to stern;
old bones like iron, unmanoeuvrable,
and little wings that clatter uselessly
as all the eggs spill out and break apart.

Then you hear them calling out their names,
crying them out dismayed, precipitate,
as if there were someone out there listening;
as if by now it's all there's left to do:

*lima fox november fox*
*charlie echo echo bravo*

and faintly

*papa india*
*papa india*
*papa india*

# Undressing

Like slipping stitches
or unmaking a bed
or rain from tiles,
they come tumbling off:
green dress, pale stockings,
loose silk – like mown grass
or blown roses,
subsiding in little heaps
and holding for a while
a faint perfume – soap,
warm skin – linking
these soft replicas of self.

And why stop there?
Why not like an animal,
a seed, a fruit, go on
to shed old layers of moult,
snakeskin, seed-husk, pelt
or hard green-walnut coat,
till all the roughnesses
of knocking age
are lost and something
soft, unshelled, unstained
emerges blinking
into open ground?

And perhaps in time
this slow undoing will arrive
at some imagined core,
some dense and green-white bud,
weightless, untouchable.
Yes. It will come,
that last let-fall of garment,
nerve, bright hair and bone –
the rest is earth,
casements of air,
close coverings of rain,
the casual sun.

# A Kosovan ghost story

Five fresh graves,
the turf rolled back
to lumpy black earth.
At each head, a stick,
a lopped branch.
This one has taken root.
Be careful where you walk,
the field may be mined.

I can hear children
playing somewhere
(as children do, no matter
what took place last week)
ahead up the green hill,
at the ragged edges of the compound
where the military are camped
with their trucks, their tents.

The soldiers speak only
to each other. They are bored
but forbidden to talk
with the villagers. And which tongue
might sound familiar, safe?
The little girls hold out
handfuls of marigolds,
then smile and run away.

From behind a lime-caulked
wall an old man peers
at the faces of strangers.
The women are hiding indoors.
They stare at each other,
at us, with eyes like dry stones,
forbidding each other to speak.
Where are the young men?

*No, there is no one here of that name.*
*In thirty years I have seen no one*
*answering to that description,*
*no children as in your photographs.*
How ordinary the lanes appear,
the mud-built houses, how
ignorant of what has
taken place inside them.

The walls are blank-eyed,
the plaster pocked and stained,
criss-crossed with holes.
Outside the grass says nothing:
the dropped flowers, the molehills,
everything is watching, silent.
The translator insists: *there is*
*no one here of that name.*

Why do they say that
nothing has happened? Why
do they think we are here, why
are the soldiers encamped at the gates,
the tent-roofs marked with a red cross,
huge, to be seen from the air?
No one enters the medical compound
to speak of the things that took place.

The women agree without words.
Drawing a shawl round a head
is enough to convey the conversation
has ended. The translator shrugs.
There is work to be done, mending
the roof, patching the windows,
filtering water. The animals must be fed.
We are not wanted. We do not understand.

*In patriarchal Muslim villages, a woman raped by an invading army is dishon-*
*oured, and shunned by her father, brothers and husband. Consequently, few are*
*willing to admit what has happened, and the true figures can only be guessed at.*

# Gitanes

They've got nothing. They do without,
spilling like oranges from the backs
of vans – no shoes, no buttons,
no towels, nothing. Just
naked children and yellow mutts.
They race down the field to the river
jumping and calling, splash over the stony beach
and into the water dressed as they are,
paint-stained blue jeans cut off at the knee,
thin cotton skirts you can see through,
their babies knotted up in scarves,
rub soap on themselves, their clothes.
That one, the dark one, he must be the prince.
He has snakes and eagles tattooed all down his back
and a beautiful woman that ripples as he moves.
He sinks below the swift black current
and the shampoo lifts from the top of his head
like a magnificent turban to drift downstream.

I cannot read my book any more and
my heart is pounding.
*T'as des cigarettes?* They stare at me
and I shake my head.
*Du feu? Rien à manger?* No.
No. No.

Now the boys turn cartwheels on the hot stones
and sing hoarse-voiced, twisting their hips to the radio
while the girls clap time in their wet blouses.
That one breaks her last cigarette in two
to share with her sister, her friend.
This one flicks her black hair forward
and combs it out with her fingers
to dry in the sun. She has streaked it with henna.
Her children chew at the end of a loaf.

I am afraid to swim in case
they steal my folded clothes, my rug,

my watch, my good book. My good life.
And the prince comes closer, smiling
in a way I cannot read.
*Tu veux danser?*
I am white, timid,
disapproving of their litter.
He takes the money I hold out silently
and tears it in pieces.
And they are laughing.
They are laughing at something.

# Emma Jones

EMMA JONES was born in Sydney, Australia in 1977. She studied English at the University of Sydney, and has sold children's clothes and car insurance, has worked at a girls' boarding school, and as an English tutor and an arts journalist. She won the Cardiff International Poetry Prize in 2003 and the Newcastle Poetry Prize, Australia's most valuable poetry prize, in 2005 for her poem 'Zoos for the Dead'. She has completed a PhD on the poet Christina Rossetti at the University of Cambridge. Emma Jones is the holder of the 2006–7 Harper-Wood Studentship in English Poetry and Literature from St John's College, Cambridge, and is the Dorothy Hewett Flagship Fellow in poetry at the Varuna Writer's Centre in New South Wales, Australia.

# Tiger in the Menagerie

No one could say how the tiger got into the menagerie.
It was too flash, too blue,
too much like the painting of a tiger.

At night the bars of the cage and the stripes of the tiger
looked into each other so long
that when it was time for those eyes to rock shut

the bars were the lashes of the stripes
the stripes were the lashes of the bars

and they walked together in their dreams so long
through the long colonnade
that shed its fretwork to the Indian main

that when the sun rose they'd gone and the tiger was
one clear orange eye that walked into the menagerie.

No one could say how the tiger got out in the menagerie.
It was too bright, too bare.
If the menagerie could, it would say 'tiger'.

If the aviary could, it would lock its door.
Its heart began to beat in rows of rising birds
when the tiger came inside to wait.

# Farming

The pearls were empire animals.
They'd been shucked from the heart of their grey mothers
which is why, so often, you'll find them
nestled at the neck and breast.
It stood to reason.
The sea was one long necklace,
and they often thought of that country.

Its customs waylaid them,
and it occupied their thoughts.
Nobody missed them.
The oysters felt nothing,
neither here nor there,
down on the farm and miles out to sea,
those swaying crops.

Rolled 'to create circumference'.
Opened to accommodate
the small strange 'foreign irritant'
that hones itself to a moon.
The oysters say
'It's a lulling stone, that outside heart
turned in, and beating.'

They knit their fields of nacre, and are quiet.
The clouds converge.
It's a sad constabulary,
the clouds and the sea, and the boats.
Because 'piracy is common'
the farmers carry guns. Does the sea
object, marshalling its edges?

Do the fish know
their glint, those inward birds
in the fields of the Pacific?
It's a singing bone,
the indivisible pearl.
It's a bright barred thing. And pearls
are empire animals. And poems are pearls.

---

# Abduction

Mother of sorrows.
How clear she is, turning the soup,
using one hand only,
while the other turns the embers of leaves and birds.
The high church spread of it –

The smoky altar –
Woods trailing off, and clicking pheasant.
All birds a variation on the peacock,
Blue fugue,
a procession of eyes and messages.

It was horrible, the wait –
the day he came, and I sat by the river.
Clenched buds
swayed in the trees like oysters.
Rotten swans

tilted their birch necks,
and it was winter
in the shored-in smoke of their throats
and the look of them,
bright and bare and branched.

The way they leaned in
was like a mirror caught off-guard.
He stood there, and thought
'Here is a thing
with clouds beaten into it,

and a sewn sky,
and newspaper clippings of strange events.'
And took me home,
and washed my eyes like rolled stones,
and ignored my mother

who shook all the fruit from the trees.
Then it was winter

for so long
that the sucked birds sang
in black and white.

Years now, or days
in the greying place,
done-up like a funny doll.
And my mother outside waiting,
sucking the sky like a cigarette.

Embers draw breath
in the flaky wind. Such acres –
If I wasn't so small
I could look for them more,
the spring-time flowers

stirring their throats,
the five-finger spread of the leaves,
and the terrible birds
that rise when my mother
cries like a whistle.


## Coin

To get by,
it had learned
the rudiments of the moon:

to wear a face
that is handled, faint;

and to walk
quietly, at night,
growing in size,
through the high and wide-paned
office buildings.

# Pastoral

It was a definite change, a migration.
It was a paring down to something lone and lashless –
autumn, a lunar season.
It moved through the traffic,
and ate early dinners in the restaurants,
and wrote letters in the afternoon.
It was like someone who saw themselves
in the mirror and got sad;
who grew their hair long, then cut it off.

The trees were honest, letting themselves go,
leaving brown eyes spread in the gutters
and a brown wind writing goodbye, goodbye.
A builder had left a radio in the rubble,
and the music moved, and the wind got a song in its head
and couldn't forget it, till the wind *was* the song,
and the wind was just something the song
had known once, and the song was worried by the gust
it felt, sometimes, inside, moving it along,
a white wave, a moving thing.

It was part of a philosophy
of things on top of other things:
the city with its greenery
and the offices built of blown paper
and the harbour that gave back its own shelved city
with the drowned in the boats of their collarbones.

Walk out a little and on the edge of the city
there are green half-fields, and buildings
in a shuttered sleep, and gathering animals.

Where it went – the other half –

(Or, just give in to it, the problem –
the coloured, colouring thing –
Newspaper report: same country, country scene.
Twenty years on, windy field, exhuming the bodies,

mass grave, trench number three: the bones
of a foetus in the bones of a woman:
'tiny bones, femurs, thighbones the size
of a matchstick'.
                    Spread babushka,
rainy season, 'the time for winnowing'.
Drowsy season. The bombs grow like blue flowers.)


## Cross Over

When they started using those gas lamps again
it was as though the fields had blinked,

or a scar had spread through the main street.
Opening time, he thought: the spread umbrella,

the takeaway shopfronts, the sea that came in
and was so cold it tried to cover itself with sand.

'Often,' he wrote, 'I can only think of warm things:
the throat of the exhaust pipe, or the belly of a whale.'

His notebook had rings of tea-stains.
After his shift he and the moon played cards.

At the pub he put fifty in the fruit machine.
'You never know,' they said, and tracked

the gas to launder the pipes, and the lights
burned blue, and he had a dream they spread

right from the road and into the sea,
and touched up its oily fleece, and spread

---

past the spokes of cars and old mermaids.
'Nothing is left of the borders,'

he thought, 'the sea and the shore', and he liked
the dream, and wrote it down.

One day he got married.
The wind was skirt-thin and the bells stuck to the sky.

They made love carefully, like scholars. She had skin
the colour of cotton, and a lisp she wore like a necklace.

'I like warm things,' he wrote, 'the smell of a spent
engine.' Outside the wind was so cold that footballs

cleaved to the wall like oysters. The hills brought
fields to the edge of the town, and the town held on

with its fingers, and, (he wrote this next part down)
*the sea was the edge to everything.*

'I've spilt
the milk,' she said, and was gone for three weeks.

'Come back,' he thought, and she did, still salty.
They kept the hobs on for warmth and watched TV.

'At night we listen for the mating calls of owls
and ambulances.' Her side of the bed was so cold

he dreamed of mackerels. Some days she'd bring
a thermos to where he worked, and watch for a bit

while the men hauled the pipes from underground,
and she felt all the gas in its stockpiles shift

the way the sea might shift, and she got sad.
This time she left a note. He found 'lunar, lunar'

written on the back of shopping lists and scratch cards.
At night he'd tread the pianola as though he were drowning.

When she got back he was careful when he cut
her suit, and her shells, and the bits of rubber

filigree she wore to ward off stingrays, so she could
never leave again. They played cards in the kitchen.

At night their bones were made of such still
things they slept alright, and dreamed of rain.


## Berlin Fugue

*for Andrew Goodwin*

It chooses its speed and direction
the collective body of the birds
its speed and direction is chosen
from the average speed and direction
this is its inner algorithm
the collective body of the birds
its speed and its rhythm is chosen
from the gestures in the wind.

Ravens, spread, or other birds –
there are hundreds above the buildings,
flying round. And no one knows
the state in which they come or land.
Not even the pickers, the feeders.
'We have come to the Unter den Linden,
and the bridges bend like branches on the water,
and the rain is on the monuments.
Like tourists we've left our memories to graze
in the high and the white places.
We're citizens of a rolling dawn.
From the air we've seen things,
the Berliner Dom

rise like a municipal building
crawled up from the sea.'

Continuous feeders –
to the birds it's all one city,
and the city is all one building,
one body of bridges and walls
and sighs and cellars and engravings.

Now the shopfronts move through the evening
and the people move through the evening
and take themselves in from the glass.

From the gestures in the wind
its speed and its rhythm is chosen
the collective body of the birds.
This is its inner algorithm.
From the average speed and direction
its speed and direction is chosen.
The collective body of the birds,
it chooses its speed and direction.

# Window

His sadness is double,
it has two edges.

One looks out –
onto skylines,
and streets with ice cream
men, and cars,
and clouds
like shirred cotton.

The other stays in
to watch
the lilies unbuckle
and the hairs
that repeat
in the washstand.

Both are impatient.
Sometimes they'll meet
and make a window.

'Look at the world!' says the glass.
'Look at the glass!' says the world.

# Gerry McGrath

GERRY MCGRATH was born in Helensburgh, near Glasgow, in 1962. He now lives in Paisley with his wife, Kate, and young son, Liam. He worked as a teacher of modern languages for some seven years, but left due to ill health in 2000. His poems have appeared in *Edinburgh Review*, *Being Alive* (Bloodaxe Books, 2005), *Painted, Spoken* and *PN Review*. Of the poems included in *New Poetries IV*, only one, 'Only Life', has been previously published.

## St Petersburg

They drink tea
in St Petersburg

remembering conversations
about truth

and if not truth
the desire for truth

and if not desire

## Itself

Who needs the genius of diffident earth?
The inborn rhythm of toppled coins?
I am closer to you than a pen to paper,
an itch to skin. Love is unthinkable.
Age, an insufficiency in itself.

# Only Life

## 1

Lint glimmers
dull in the baubled wool;
laundered stars unsparkled
blink on
off          on

## 2

In a voice
surprised
by its own remoteness
my father not knowing
he was entering
his final month
winked
cigarette
butt clamped
in the jaws of his fingers
and said
*precisely*

*precisely*

as if there was something
extraordinary
absolutely extraordinary
and memorable
about this
his only life.

# Anstruther

How, where, does it begin?
In the head? With the
extremities? You countable,
lovable digits, you fingers, toes,
are you where it all starts?
Make a note: the train leaves
at 9.10 in the morning,
for a city in a valley. I don't
know its name, who lives there.
No one does. There are old stories.
Many have lived remarkable lives.

Sawdust beach, amber moon,
sea moss, sifting herons,
lemony lime, piglet spill,
crimson rock pools reflecting
things beyond reflection.

We fish for others.
We trespass.
We are beloved.


# Element

The sea –
a sweet, blue history
of the Earth.

And gravity –
the soil's otherness,
pulse of the crowd felt
in an empty room.

# Whispers

From a table; lone, polished, walnut table with history, I unhook
and hook eyes on the drowsy sailcloth of your skin, watch you
walking in the shadowless hall, clothes for the basket, hesitating.
And what I would like to do is part company with this dreary chair,
get up, hold you, kiss you, but outside a wind is busy piling leaves
against the gable, rain's whispering in the dark, and the promise
of what might be is looking back at us through a doorway with eyes
like wet, black earth.

# The Colour of Water

On glassy Turnberry beach
we went looking
for a world without stars.
From sand you magicked
a castle; moat, portcullis,
ramparts, turrets
i.e. the lot
while my cheap feet made
do with carving the date
and our names
beside a feathery burn.

See, poetry, what you can do
when you try?
If I was feeling brave, poetic,
painterly, I might say:
take one potato (halved)
a few watercolours
and attempt to draw
this threesome –

hand that weighs, judges
man's equine shiver
a charnel house of shells.

## The Language of Pines

Here again, yes here, touched,
yes, by the future. Let me say

how we progressed down the hill
stepping from fog to visibility.

Listen, these eyes, heat, more-
than-blood warmth, feel

the minute forgiveness of rain,
unconfessable love, salt,

hear the language of pines,
soft bleating as of a child
all

the painstaking increments
of our descending.

# Loose Ends

*for Czeslaw Milosz*

A messy routine today.
I read a short poem
that takes some forgiving.
He is gone now.

My father drifts to mind
grey face leaking hope
that all the loose ends
will finally be gathered in.

# Magic

He spent years thinking
how he wished never
to see the word on the page
hear its opposing voice nor
think of the space given it.
Then suddenly Yes's Opposite
conjuring all manner of things
as if by magic a future.

## Soft Tissue

From this low brae, a holding
station where shadows of cloud are all
that crosses the snow, I hear
the speech marks of tenderness
that unravel you, a too-demanding
fear of nothing changing suddenly
changing into beauty and weightlessness,
while your face, soft tissue
of your beginning and your ending,
tilts at an unknown future, a forgotten past.

## The Photographer

We see things
you and I –

orange beech leaves

hills

the skin of a pool

a lighthouse beam

of frost.

## Summer's End

is a hill
bleared by rain

a first trembling
wind

the memory
that into autumn's room
winter will dip a glass &

hold up darkness
to a chittering lantern
moon.

# Kei Miller

KEI MILLER was born in Jamaica in 1978. He read English at the University of the West Indies and completed an MA in Creative Writing at Manchester Metropolitan University. His work has appeared in journals such as *Kunapipi*, *Parnassus* and *The Caribbean Writer*. His first collection of short fiction, *The Fear of Stones* (Macmillan, 2006), was shortlisted for the Commonwealth Writers' First Book Prize in 2007 and his first poetry collection, *Kingdom of Empty Bellies*, was published in 2006 by Heaventree Press. He is the editor of Carcanet's *New Caribbean Poetry: An Anthology* (2007). He has been a visiting writer at York University in Canada and the Department of Library Services in the British Virgin Islands, and a Vera Ruben Fellow at Yaddo.

# How we became the pirates

In this country you have an accent;
in the pub, a woman mocks it.
You want to ignore her but wonder
how many hearts is she being bold for?
Hate, in this place,
is restrained as the landscape,
buried, usually, under a polite 'cheers, mate'.
And what a thing to mock –
the way we shape words differently.
But maybe it's the old colonial hurt
of how we became the pirates, dark people
raiding English from the English,
stealing poetry from the poets.
So English poetry is no longer from England.
You swear – *Lady, if I start a poem*
*in this country*
*it will not be yours.*

# Hope in that darkness

In this country, plantains do not ripen
naturally. You must place them on windowsills
wrapped in newspaper, and only hope
in that darkness they grow softer
and sweet.

# The only thing far away

In this country, Jamaica is not quite as far
as you might think. Walking through Peckham
in London, West Moss Road in Manchester,
you pass green and yellow shops
where tie-headwomen bargain over the price
of dasheen. And beside Jamaica is Spain
selling large yellow peppers, lemon to squeeze
onto chicken. Beside Spain is Pakistan, then Egypt,
Singapore, the world ... here, strangers build home
together, flood the ports with curry and papayas;
in Peckham and on Moss Road, the place smells
of more than just patty or tandoori. It smells like
Mumbai, like the Castries, like Princess Street, Jamaica.
Sometimes in this country, the only thing far away
is this country.

# Your dance is like a cure

In this country, on a Saturday night
you are usually the best dancer;
it was not so back home.
Here you can dance
dances that have fallen out
of season, like mangoes in February
or guineps at Christmas. It does not matter
in this new country;
they do not know Spanish Town Road,
have never danced into the headlights
of early morning buses… though,
neither have you; you were never skilled
enough back there. You never entered
the middle circle – like a Holy of Holies –
where only good dancers dared venture.
But in this country, you move like fire
amongst the cane, you move like sugar
and like ocean; they say – you are the sharp
swing of a cutlass, they say –
you are like ointment in a deep wound.
They say your dance is like a cure.

# In Praise of the Contribution of Pots

This poem, a eulogy for Florence Bygrave
who died and was buried simply, without
poppies, no marching band to trumpet the glory
of the twelve pots she donated.
For after giving two sons to the war,
the telegrams announcing their never-coming-back
like thin tombstones in her bureau drawer,
who could have asked her to give more?
But when there were no tanks left in Britain,
Florence answered the call for iron –
ran into the road to deliver
unto that passing, rattling heap, all her pots!
O, Florence, for whom till her dying day
no one gave a medal, praise the sacrifice you made,
the meat from your cellar that all went to rot.
I will tell you now, it was worth it –
that a tank was built from the silver melt
of your cookware. And all the boys
who drove thought they were dreaming
when the smell of simmering onions would arise, the sweet morning
aroma of pork sausages. You gave
those boys not only walls, but the metallic fact
of a mother's kitchen calling them home.
In every war, praise the contribution of women,
O praise Florence's contribution of pots.

# Hurricane Story 2004

*after Olive Senior*

It was the year Miss Millie gave the children back
to their father and started to paint; the year
the neighbour said she was mad, for which mother
would trade her flesh for canvases and oil?

The children worried – it was the youngest boy
who found her on a nightstand, squeezing
tubes of makeup onto the bare wall. And when
Miss Millie saw that she was seen, she jumped

off screaming, packed all three boys' belongings
into an old fruit box and left them at the door
of Lenroy's apartment, saying, 'Please,
please. Just for a while.'

It was the year the deejay became popular
leading the people to dance thunderclap, lightning
and hard rain – so much danger in movements
that seed clouds and beg wind. It was the year

Miss Millie started giving her name as simply
Millicent. The year she started to dance again,
to smile again. Though when the hurricane struck
it took the roof from Millie's workshop.

All night the room filled up with dark
water, and she woke to find her canvases were soft
and meaningless; to find the divorce papers floating
by an overturned easel, the signatures spread

into nothing. It was the year Miss Millie landed
unto the floor with a splash, water risen to her face,
and she laughed and she cried, though in all that wet
who could tell the difference?

# The Candle We Made

Even before you called to say
there was no light in Jamaica
and the candle we made the night
before I left was lit,
I was already up
remembering how we stood
by our small stove and melted
white wax with blue crayons,
poured it in a low glass to set.
In this place, a far
too-early sun had risen –
so even before the phone rang
and I dived for your voice,
I was already up, and your face
was flickering into view.

# An Allowance for Ula-May

Ula-May, keeper, interpreter and dispenser
of rules, read the Book of Leviticus once a month.
She believed only in laws that forbade,
none that allowed, so she did-not
more than she ever did.
Consider, that on quiet days
bowed on her red floor and committed
to the slow shining circles of a coconut husk –
even in that safe holiness she did not
let go of things inside. She did not hum,
no spiritual, no sankey, no complaint
of arthritis ever passed her lips.
Consider, that even when dying
from unknown sickness,
she would not consult the obeah woman.

Ula-May, great-grandmother,
I write for you now an allowance
as rules that once were, have withered.
The page of this poem is a space
on which you may throw rice grains as divination
use up the magic that rotted
inside you. Between these words,
a rhythm, that you may tie your head tonight,
probably for the first time, let your hips go
where they have wanted. The heart of this
is love, Ula-May, which you may take whole,
turn it towards your awful self. Such things,
like the love of skin, the love of what we bring
to this world, are no longer forbidden.
They are permissible, they are allowed; you may.

# The Discovered Ark

The first real proof will be shells
and a deposit of salt
found somewhere on Everest:
it is unlikely men would climb,
their knapsacks full of clams
sea water in their flasks.

The second will be a rotting hull
crashed far from any sea.
Beside it, a fig tree,
and buried there –
the perfect fossil of a dove.

But all along, every tribe
has told the single story
of a flooded earth, a great canoe. All along,
the name of Noah has been large
as the name of God.
And is it not frightening, the possible proof –
it is not faith, but an anger
that moved the mountains?

# *from* The Broken (II)

## I

A worm broken in two will become two.
Broken in a hundred, it shall become a hundred.
Then, are we not like worms
that started whole, but have become
multiple, legion, broken.

## IV

And maybe it is the only way we see,
as if the world exists in a clay jar.
We are always groping; we recognise each other
only dimly; in our meetings
there is often night between us.
My love, I try to see you with fingertips
and with my ears. I hang to the shape
of your cheekbones and the sound
of your sighs. But we exist in clay;
broken is the only way light will enter.
On that day we see each other
wholly. You undress me. I say,
this is my body – it is for you.

## V

Borders are jagged; every island is proof.
Straight lines on a map are decisions made by men
who knew nothing of mountains or lakes or the spread
of aunts and uncles, or of language.
There are Indians in South America
who cross countries each day without visas,
no knowledge of a line where flags change.
Every world elides into another and nothing
is straight or easy – *the world don' go so.*

*That is lie.* My love, if we struggle at first
to fit our chests and our legs together
it is only natural. We are different
islands, our borders salted differently.
Love is how our skin breaks against each other,
how we bleed into each other, and how
we heal.


## VI

Broken is the shape of everything
like yesterday
                              like memory

now is so large
                    the present is everywhere:
we break them into pieces

and they are all we have
                    they are all we carry into tomorrow:
                                        broken bits

it is the shape            of everything
like our anointing
                    an alabaster jar is broken

that each step into Jerusalem would be fragrant
that our crudest signatures stamped into mud

might have      rising from them      a year's wages
worth of scent    though our spirits
                          would be shattered

                          though our backs
                                    and our bones
                                        would be rubble.

Broken is the shape and shade
                              of everything
like our patched-up dreams that once were whole

now we hold on
                simply
                        to its largest remnant

        we squeeze so tight our hands bleed

the holding of every dream
                              is a crucifixion.

And broken is the final shape of everyone

it is the only way we could become
                who we are

by breaking

out of                        into

                        consider now, the evidence:
            scattered shells
                    halves of cocoons, doors
torn from their hinges,
                    windows flung and cracked
                            against the stump of trees,
walls like centuries discarded –
consider the dust that once was skin
                        consider the cotton we outgrew
consider shoes and their eventual mouths

but still we stand with ruined feet
                in this world of splinters,
        our skin scraped raw by our emerging

                    we have been bruised
into ourselves.

# Christopher Nield

CHRISTOPHER NIELD was born in London in 1974, studied English Literature at the University of Leeds, and later gained a Masters degree in Modernist Literature at the University of Cambridge. He works in London as a copywriter. Since 2005 he has contributed a weekly poetry column to *The Epoch Times*, and is completing his first collection of poems. His poetry has been accepted for publication by *Ambit*, *Chroma*, *The Liberal*, *PN Review* and *The Rialto*. In 2006 he was one of the winners of the Keats–Shelley Prize.

# Two Cardinals Painted by El Greco

This asymmetric choreography
Of hands forbids the pausing eye to sink
A man's anachronistic poverty
In catechising certainties of pink.

Lush fingers sag as if to drag suspense,
Though others snare the second to a chair.
A beard is tersely flaring to offence;
The hat will spare its caring, debonair,

Administrator. His shaggier father's
Knuckles curl on the vulgar book, his own,
Yet a flat reverential palm avers
That love is not a law to be alone.

So could we burn the saint who mistranslated
That horns blazed from the humbled prophet's head?

# The Difference You Make

I have a sad genius for stasis:
The bleep, the severed sleep, the Circle line.
The difference you make is difference itself.

I trace the tidy magic of design
And stare in admiration at the sky.
The bleep, the severed sleep, the Circle line.

I down some paracetamol and cry
Love is disappointment's broken solace
And stare in admiration at the sky.

Dare we stir the certain into crisis?
The vision tempts too late, pre-empts the pain.
Love is disappointment's broken solace

To disembark at Temple cleansed by rain.
But you and I both in the dark confess
The vision tempts too late, pre-empts the pain.

Don't stress the question and I won't say yes –
I have a sad genius for stasis –
But you and I both in the dark confess
The difference you make is difference itself.

# What It's Like, After All

I have discovered love;
You weren't what I expected.
Your paunch, for example,
Isn't – let's be honest –
The ideal.

And yet I have found rest on it.
Just touching it –
That unfettered belly,
That soft underside
Of your adamantine suit –
Is utter joy –
Cold fluttering lightness.

I have discovered faith
In your folds, those august
Fistfuls of too-muchness,
That smooth interior
All over, all over!
My caramel, sheer, irresistible Ganesha.

I have discovered lust
In your feet,
Those fascinated dainty snubs at which far point your body ends
And curves up to begin
All over again.

I have discovered trust
In your technique:
Ten out of ten.

I have discovered home
In your grip,
The way you fashion me
With hands, so delectably unseen,
When you allow yourself
To quicken from prim majesty
And, afterwards, on my chest
You sleep. That fat, elusive
Upward flicker
Of grace
At your imperious mouth
Astounds me – agonises
My lank heart.

# Aphrodite

This throat is white as the water's fur –
The long white stretch to the tethered skull –
The bare white pulse
Open to the outcast stare –
That life –
That beating there.

That silent curl –
The wreath around the base,
The marble scruff –
Plumes with fearsome colour
Simple carelessness,
The perfect whiteness
Of the figure, here,
And gives his form
A certain
Cut –

A beauty – not that
Statuesque stain
Of bodies embarrassed by the life they train –
The life that can contain
Such pain.

This throat is cold
To the imagined touch.
Unflushed, unstirred,
The owner cannot hear
The world that tries to desecrate
Such graceful hate

(A callousness
Of flesh, in such
Vicious
Natural reign.)

He is only half aware
Of the peaceful, helpless stare –
The wake of expectation, where
Volition fearful
In the feet that move
Will prove
The viscera of another loss.

An emblem of certain
Failure –
The sterile suppleness
Of the body
Standing
So assuredly –
The station of the figure
The world
Tries to possess.

Perceive the scene:
The sculptural
Mass of random hair.
Conceive
The simple humanness
Of something
So opaque to sense:
The fleshy screen
That hides all signs
Of being close
To us,

The informal progress
That shows
The hard disparity
With others hideous,

The hands bound
To touching
Quick insentience.

# Kay's Song

A disconnecting lens stuck in my eye.
I ran away, a breathing ghost of frost
Upon the lake of thought I could not drown.

The Snow Queen promised love beyond the gate.
The Christ-child lay among the goldenrod.
I ran away, a breathing ghost of frost.

I saw forever in a blade of ice
The rigor mortis of her blue embrace.
The Christ-child lay among the goldenrod.

Stark fingers scratched this silver alphabet,
But never carved the absence of my wound,
The rigor mortis of her blue embrace.

Light's elemental void was green as blood
And glared to comfort me against desire,
But never carved the absence of my wound.

The winter palace, my eternal test,
A disconnecting lens stuck in my eye
And glared to comfort me against desire
Upon the lake of thought I could not drown.

The mirror trickled clear. I tasted salt.
I ran away, a breathing ghost of frost,
For there you were, my true and fearless bride
And there we lay among the goldenrod.

# Sancreed

This is the green world, though now it is grey.
The sky is white, nothing but white and rain.
The rain resolves into redundant day
As I trudge up the path towards the plain
Petition of the cross. I cannot pray.
God and the Devil are beyond the sane.
No tourist loiters near. No hand has known
A twist of sticks and hay to praise the stone.

The grassway turns and its sly gravity
Tugs my blood into the grove. Soaked and slow,
There stands a ring of pines and there the holly
Shines an ornate glass calm of spikes. A sparrow
Stabs its fierce alarm – a faint, frantic pity.
Here, here is the well in its granite hollow.
Its moss-green eye glares up, implacable.
I am unprepared. I possess no ritual.

Here the gifts are given, the wishes made:
Condoms, coins, cards, hair. But these passport faces
Fade, blue with kisses, under branches strayed
By clouties: rags, ribbons, string, shoelaces
All tied. Each cross a sign of life betrayed
By fear, by calling elemental graces –
From candles, mud, thin air – to come and bless
The moment's damage and forgetfulness.

What stirs the stagnant mind to say goodbye
And not despair? I shut my eyes and stare.
Somehow I see no black, no back of eye,
A breath between the eye and its skin lair,
Somehow a sense of space, a sense of why –
Between the cross and well, their nagging care,
Unastonished by superstitious dread –
I am the sun in a cosmos of red.

# Joanna Preston

JOANNA PRESTON was born in 1972 in Sydney, Australia and currently lives in Christchurch, New Zealand. She has dabbled in jobs as various as plant-waterer for a garden centre, trackwork rider for a racehorse trainer and librarian's assistant, and was commissioned to write a promotional song for a sporting event. She left Australia for New Zealand to marry her scientist husband and has lived in Christchurch ever since, apart from a three-year stint from 2003 to 2006 living in West Yorkshire, England, and studying for an MPhil in Creative Writing from the University of Glamorgan, Wales. She has edited/co-edited three New Zealand poetry anthologies, and is currently co-editing a fourth: an anthology of Australasian haibun.

Preston's work has appeared in a number of publications in Australia, New Zealand and Britain.

# The hill paddock

Searching for the missing calf
in the brittle light of winter afternoon

we found instead
a tuft of bloodied feathers
fluttering in the ryegrass

as though they could remember flight,
and longed for it.

# Curly Hill Road

Walking back to an empty house
through the dusk of that first summer
I watched pipistrelles hunting
their high, thin calls like the chink
of ice-glazed tinsel,
as they flung themselves after moths
pivoting midair
on the point of an elbow
as though skin could stretch indefinitely,
as though bones never snapped.

# Lighthouse-keeper

I've strewn kelp and sea lettuce over the metal stairs
– she'll like that. Even the walls smell of her.

When night spreads to extinguish the land
I put this lighthouse to her work,

pick out fishing boats and container ships
infesting the sea like lice in a seal's pelt.

I send them onto the rocks, vessels filled
with the cold weight of my devotion.

Afterwards, she sings to me
in a voice so high I can barely hear.

She left me a gift once – a femur
studded with barnacles where her lips had rested.

I lean from the railing and imagine letting go,
feel my body smash a path through the thick air

I've almost forgotten the point of a day-lit sky.
I wake at sunset drenched, and sticky with the salt taste of her.

# Gloves

Great-Grandmother's gloves were kept for funerals,
in tissue paper, limp as something stillborn.

She drew them on slowly, the grey silk
of the other self she wore.

Through each service they lay folded
on her lap, water-stained wings of a moth.


Afterwards, she gives them to me
to put away, still warm, and marked
where her wedding band has worn to gold wire.

She slides the long pins out of her hair,
and I brush until it hangs, a fall
of frozen water down her spine.

She sends me to the garden for fresh flowers
and sits for a while, just visible through the open door,
straight-backed and still, with naked hands.

# Parable of the Drought

He got up from the narrow bed
and shaved off his beard,
rinsing his face and the razor
with a last mugful of fresh water.
He dressed, and waited
for sunlight through the window
to wake the boy.

They walked all morning,
following the sun and the line
of fenceposts that shimmered west.
He looked only once at the sky,
shading his eyes
when a black cockatoo flew overhead.

When they came to broken country
the bloodwood and gidgee
sucked the shade back into themselves.
Heat smashed against the gibbers.

He kissed the boy's forehead
and held his skinny shoulders,
breathing his scent of smoke and dust and sweat
and a sweetness
that for a moment could have been his wife.
He slid his fingers into the boy's hair
– *just like a wether*, he thought, *just like a ewe* –

He watched until the boy's eyes
lost their brilliance – the same brittle blue
as the sky that even now
refuses to cloud.

# The bull sale

One by one the bulls muscle in
like nightclub bouncers
– all balls and beard, or rather
all balls and back-end.

The auctioneer wipes the sweat
from his face. Hands flash
and the bids charge and climb
to clash in the air
above the sawdust and bull shit.

A tight-skinned bull,
scrotum swinging
in the centre of it all – a god
in bull's form, his forehead a thick plate
of bone, hard as a butcher's block.

# Skeleton

To hurl your own bones
skull first
down a twisting
chine of ice,

on a dinner tray
balanced
on two steel blades

this
is free-fall,
air banked
like snow,

rime on the lip
of high, sharp bends,
teeth an inch
from the ice

speed is bled
into frozen walls,
skin shaking rush
toe-steered,

body straight
a falcon's stoop

the thin pane
of fontanelle,
a pulse, to be
unborn again

but ready this time,
headfirst
and down

into the cold,
the brilliant
light.

*Skeleton sledding: a sport similar to luge except for the position on the sled,
which is prone rather than supine, head first rather than feet first.*

# Gabriel

A boy with hair like sand in the rain,
cropped to cup the bones
of his skull as closely as the priest

who, with three palmfuls of water
washed him from his mother's body,
into the kingdom of his name.

# The damaged

Against a backdrop of lost Atlantis
they come, one after the other
in chariots of steel and webbing –
a beautiful boy with an emptied face,
a gaunt girl with a thick black mane
whose hands beat and beat the air, escaping,
a child with a sharp crooked spine,
limbs tangled like mangrove roots.

Grown men lift them from their chairs,
bear them into the pool, light
as petals in their arms – the damaged
children with lotus faces, who slip free
of their bodies into the water, and blossom.

# *from* Venery

## i   The Pride of Lions

But before we could marry, he became a lion –
thick pelted, and rich with the musk of beast.

The switch to all fours was not easy – all his weight
slung from the blades of his shoulders.
His deltoids knotted like teak burls,
and I burnished them as he slept.

Burrs matted his mane, and for days
he wouldn't let me groom him –
slapped me away with a suede paw,
snarled against my throat.

He would not eat fruit, or drink milk,
but tore meat from the bones I provided.

His claws caught in the carpet,
so I stripped the rugs from the floor
and polished the boards until they gleamed
and rang with the chime of his nails.

I stroke his saffron hide
and tangle my fingers deep in his ruff,
draw him up around me, ardent
as the gleam of his topaz eyes

– the hypnotic lash of his tail,
the rasp of his tongue on my thighs.

## ii   A Knot of Toads

We sweated and couldn't sleep.
Darkness purred from a hundred throat-sacs,
a generator left to chug itself to death.

Next morning Aunty's gardening shoes
were sticky-toed and glistening.
*They'll fuck anything*, Daniel said,
and I learnt a new word
fishing a cane toad out of the pool.

It lay on its back in a puddle,
an old fencing glove brought to life, to hunger
for something I didn't understand.

That night we snuck out in our undies
with a torch to watch them, all
splotchy yellow eyes and warty backs,
climbing each other.

Daniel's skin was smooth, his breath
ragged against my neck.

# Edward Ragg

EDWARD RAGG was born in 1976 in Stockton-on-Tees. A scholar of Keble College, Oxford and Selwyn College, Cambridge, he holds degrees in English, Publishing and American Literature. In 2005 he completed a PhD on the work of Wallace Stevens at Cambridge, where he also taught from 2001 to 2006. As a Fellow of the Rothermere American Institute, he co-organised with Bart Eeckhout the first major UK conference devoted to Stevens. He subsequently co-edited with Eeckhout a special issue of *The Wallace Stevens Journal* (Spring 2006) and is the editor of a volume of essays, *Wallace Stevens across the Atlantic*, and the author of a forthcoming study of Stevens. In addition to publishing poems in *Agenda*, *PN Review*, *Critical Quarterly* and other magazines, he works as a wine educator and wine judge. He lives in Beijing, where he teaches at Tsinghua University and is the founder of a wine consultancy with his wife, Fongyee Walker.

# Narco Poem

## I

Because the air was night he lay on his bed,
And, as his wife dozed in the duvet, converted
Her heavier breathing into stanzas of sleep.

And as he lay awake sleeping, another poet
Rose from his side, not vividly like a movie,
Nor grey like slumbering ghosts. He sat on the bed,

Looked once into the whites of the eyes, peered
Into the black pupils, then walked out of the room,
Through the corridor and down into the study.

He sat at the poet's desk and at every bench
The poet had sat, just as he would sleep in
Every bed the poet slept, and wrote silver lines.

He wrote a poem about an insomniac whose
Sleep, as his wife lay breathing, was a poetry
Awake, yet dreaming of sleep. It was the dream

His wife had dreamt and dictated in her breath,
The breath he heard in the first poem he wrote:
That one kissing a girl in a churchyard at night.

The silver lines were silver because the ink was so.
They were not a poetic after-touch, half make-believe,
Half novel story told after the dream was dreamt.

He wrote the poem as he sat and in one sitting
Told exactly of the poet in the room, and of his wife,
How between them they could have written

Any poem had they forgotten the past, the first girl
In the churchyard, the way the moon was not drunk,
But that the man was, screaming in her ear all night.

There was not a silver lining. It took five minutes
To write, or what had seemed only five. He folded
The paper, sealed the envelope, left no autograph.


## II


That morning the insomniac sifted his papers,
Scrabbling for the scraps he had made yesterday
Morning, or the morning after that. He was convinced

He had forgotten the lines about his wife's breathing.
He could never remember the slightest syllable of what
He'd said, of what he dreamt he'd write if only he'd meant.

Then there it was, the narco poem, sealed and meant.
He took it to the post-box, though it had no address.
He could not find his pen, so posted it instead.

The narco poem delivered itself to the entire world.
Da Xiang, in Beijing, fell asleep from the first page.
Lou Dodds, Sydney, snored his way through stanza eight.

Tedman Littwin, Deerfield, Mass., nodded off before
His wife read the post, and when she opened the
Envelope watched her own fingers turn silver

Before her eyelids closed. She had heard and understood
The writings of ghosts. It was how the poem spoke.
How the night talkers burbled to their wives,

How the sleepwalkers carried it as they folded their
Husbands' clothes, or put the cat out for the night.
Symposia entitled 'Sleep And Poetry' filled

The lecture halls and hoards of sleeping students
Lay in the benches as lecturers snored. Then critics
Wrote drowsy notes on the sleeping poem's sound.

Only the insomniac's wife dreamt peacefully. She knew
He would never write a poem without her snores, that
Had he dreamt the other poet by himself there would

Never be a silver line or verse. His page was black and
Black because he would never sleep. He lay awake himself.
And the other poet, nodding, laid his head down on the desk.

## A Side of Gravadlax

Orange-pink fillet slipped from its vacuum pack,
Sinews and scent of dill, crystals of salt and sugar,
A knife so sharp its blade can neither slide nor slip.

Then debates of serving like lovers' tiffs: lemon
No lemon, rocks of black pepper, a dusting of cayenne,
Sandwich sheets or box-cut 'sashimi' strips.

This fish, caught in Scotland, cured as the Scandinavians
Preserve, freighted to Oxford, pressed in my winter hands,
Then driven two and a half hours home in a car as cold

As the December night, is part of the love for which
We hunger, one of all the sides of your desire:
Its fibrous oils a longing, its buxom flesh a carnival.

# The Parochial Man

## I

The grass I see is greener than they say
Far away. The truth is at my picket-fence
And settles for no more than border sense.

The world is wide, I know, but do not think
My mind is only local: it is parochial.
These parishes are of a piece with any soul.

Whether I stand in Chongqing or the Yukon,
Some plot of Arkansas or New South Wales,
Whether the wind is Ural or dust of Gobi gales,

Whether my bowl clunks in Xi'an, my platter
Scrapes the table of a Piemonte town, I am
The universal person within the same man.

## II

It is not the parish but parishes I seek;
And yet I lost my son who finds this place
Backward and banal, a region without trace

Of cultivation, save for the tilled earth.
My wife, perhaps a Puritan maid, as dead
As him, or deader, by all the epitaphs I read.

Perhaps he sits in a café in Rapallo, supposing
The navel of the world his, never knowing
The local is never global and never going

Anywhere, for all his books and travel, outside
An unmoving self. I have toured the ways of age.
I found his final words mannered: faisandé.

## III

So spoke the parochial man. But then
A storyteller came to town, an itinerant soul,
But no less parochial. He talked in the
Living parishes wherever they were local.

A crowd gathered at the picket-fence. The man
Peered at the storyteller as if he saw himself:
'Suppose I call you A,' the teller turned to him,
'And tell the tale of A as if it were truth itself.'

The parochial man nodded but stood his ground,
His mind full of gypsies and bustling towns,
A scarlet letter stamped into the dust, a tale
Of the last son lost… The storyteller began:

'A lived all his life about the picket-fence.
C, his friend, came over nights to talk and drink.
They took a little bourbon, but mostly beer,
Recounted tales around the kitchen sink.'

'Then C told A of the most enchanting girl,
A foreigner, B, who'd come to heave the jugs
In a tavern where no respecting man would tread.
A and C were quiet and stared into their mugs.'

'What happened? Did B fall between them,
Or A fight C for B, the rival queen, the realm
Around the picket-fence? All we know is this:
A packed a trunk and laid it underneath his bed.'

## IV

The parochial man was silent still. The crowd
Frittered and fell to seed the limiting earth.
He stood in his room and heaved out the case
Behind the trunk he'd meant to leave in place.

Bound for Rapallo: there the trunk would sit
And C would discover it, unlocked, unlived,
Of what he'd leave to the memory of each: that
Puritan maid, that fence, that dismal light;

And to B, who'd told a few stories herself,
And for C who'd heard almost all he could,
His heart bound for A, not B, at least not then.
Their triangle stayed isosceles the further he ran.

To Rapallo, where his son would already leave,
Would show that side of the parochial men
The other parishes they had always dreamed
Beyond Rapallo, beyond the name of any town

Or part of sea, or lighthouse, bunker, cave,
The innermost shells of molluscs, be they limpet
Or clam. To see how the villages look from up
Above: the native fields, the flowers in them.

## Contract Killer

### I

The afternoon died in paper. The corpses sat
In the living room, perched on bar stools,
Leaned casually with one arm against the walls;

Not cadavers in the kitchen, heaped high and
Blood on the tiles, the murderer dressed in a
Redcoat, one head lying in a macabre hand.

They lay in familiar poses, watching the game,
Clasping a beer, reclining on the balcony with
A glass of wine, eyeing the market stalls below.

The TV broadcast a live show from somewhere.
Death, like paternity, is a legal fiction. At least
It must be certified. Not that they had died,

But that, in dying, were bound. The murderer
Opened his briefcase, took out his forms,
Removed the papers from the corpses' mouths.


## II


Their consent was blood, and without that signature
He'd have his work cut out. It was true. They had
Let themselves be killed. He had agreeable, even

Boyish looks, knew how to dismantle every lock.
But they had let themselves, just a little or a lot.
It made the legal side a little hard to disprove.

How often had they died, he thought, sitting
At their sides. Old murderers clunked obols
In their cloaks: each closed lid paid for itself.

There was always a pleasant send-off, casting away,
Crossing the dark river. The metaphors were
Content with their jobs and the murderers too.

Now there were so many short-term contracts.
It was an honour to be occupied, devise the
Script, always be at home when least suspected.

But the work-load scarcely left him time to live.
It was a world of envy in which they died,
Or just dropped off when they hadn't the heart.

No one slept. It was pure neglect. Here he is
In the back seat at the traffic lights, thinking:
Why do they forget to bleed before they die?

It's hardly natural, the murderer said.
And here he is again in an aeroplane:
The stewardess and the husband trying,

Trying so damn hard to live one more time.
Before the plane touches down they sign their names,
Their contracts muddled with the landing cards.


### III

His briefcase was full. He sipped the wine,
Stepped off the balcony, alighted in the square.
How much admiration he had for the living live:

They were here, plucking chickens, and the
School teacher closing her books, roasting
A bird in the back of her mouth. She is raw

And ripe: and here. It gives him an appetite.
But, being perpetually in season, she misses death.
She signs papers with her hand, not her mouth.

How he envies the different murderer to whom
She will capitulate. How she eats away at his appetite.
How delectable, for all that, the chickens smell.


### IV

He was tired now. One more form could fit
In his case, always one. The TV blaring, the crowd
Cheering, the woman who stops watching her son:

He let them go. They can go (the paper a little
Sodden with saliva now). Is it permissible in
A contract of this remit to give them leave?

Is it the dying live that decide or the murderer
Who lets them kill? He could not decide.
The afternoon was old and the briefcase full.

He would go home to his wife and live just
A little that night. Here they are now, curling up.
Later, a little later, she takes the paper from his mouth.

## Last Look at the Stars

### Libra

Don't let your lack of enthusiasm for a certain project
Deter you from giving it your best. No matter how uninspiring
It currently looks, it does stand a very good chance of
Bringing rewards or kudos in the future. With alternative
Therapies and lifestyles especially well-starred just now,
You can afford to start thinking along more imaginative
Lines. Everything happens for a reason, which is why
You should pay particular attention to a faraway voice
Or influence over the next few days. Don't forget:
Getting it right is as important as getting it done.

### Pisces

A team effort or enterprise should start to show results
This week reminding you of why you got involved
In the first place. It now seems that the sooner you steer
Your life on to a less exclusive footing, the better it will
Be for all concerned. Don't be afraid to reposition any
Goal posts hindering your movements. With today's
New Moon adding insight to any negotiations, and
Eloquent Mercury moving in your favour, you should
Be able to outwit opposition at every turn. Much has to do
With looking confident: so practise, in advance, if necessary.

# Owl and Cat: A Lesson

*These forms are not abortive figures, rocks,*
*Impenetrable symbols, motionless. They move*

*About the night.*

> Wallace Stevens, 'The Owl in the Sarcophagus'

Bookshelves and spines: nouns of the celebrated dead
Now gold once more as the lamps of the classroom shine,
As the afternoon light thins and, fading, plays;

That passage from Shelley's *Defence*, our tired faces
Stretched far from those 'eternal regions' where the
'Owl-winged faculty of calculation dare never soar',

As if the poet stood in the corner fuming, in one hand
A tattered manuscript, in the other a bird of prey;
The silence as our brows crumple, our eyelids fall.

Then the long walk home where the lamps gleam
Bumper to bumper and the winter moon surveys
Its obvious tenure, unwatched and new.

Suddenly, in a familiar street an owl calls. I stand
Stiller than the black cat who perches on a fence
And listens, as if by pausing here all three of us

Could elope and sail away for a year and a day,
As if with runcible spoons we might eat our fills
Or the cat and owl lullaby under my moon-like gaze.

This is not dark scholar's bird, half-moon specs surveying
A tawny breast, no more than cat must be Egyptian deity.
Owl, hint your hooting: only you pronounce *magnificat*.

---

# Philip Rush

PHILIP RUSH was born in 1956 in Middlesex but has now lived for most of his life in Gloucestershire, where he has worked as a teacher for many years. He plays the electric violin and remains a committed supporter of West Ham United, despite everything. His poetry has been published in magazines in both Britain and the USA, including *The Rialto, Poetry Review* and *Miller's Pond*. In 2000 he won the Ledbury Poetry Competition with his poem 'Percebes'. He has completed the diploma in creative writing at Bristol University.

# Custom

For all intents and purposes now,
daylight is perpetual,
the midnight moon
purely decorative
and our bonfires superfluous.

The potatoes are flowering
in the village allotments
and it has become obligatory
to use headlights when driving
along the lane beneath the epileptic trees.

The tradition here
is that the children catch crows
with long-handled nets
and mount them on garden canes
before running through the village,

bearing them aloft,
the wings flapping weakly
in a parody of flight, and never quite
in time with the melancholy
ceremonial music the adults play.

Visitors are politely restrained
with elegant silk ropes,
sold toffee and burnt cider,
discouraged
from wandering into the woods.

# Tuareg

I have decided to join the Tuareg.
I have sent away for full details
and an application form, enclosing an s.a.e.

The things you're most attached to,
they're the ones you need the least,
as Bob Dylan says, or more or less.

I will soothe my face with exotic cloth,
dyed in some distant indigo souk.
My skin will take on that interesting blue.

I will spit at the price of camels.
I will master the nose-flute
if the nose-flute is one of their instruments.

(Sources are rather vague about this.)
Already I'm more than half in love,
about 85% I'd estimate,

with the women, with their long-suffering
beauty & their premature ageing;
and with the men's devout and communal

solitude, their myths about rain,
the astronomical lore they're steeped in,
the confusion between desert and sea.

I am prepared to undertake a name change,
sacrificing maybe a ram, slitting its throat.
(I'm making a lot of this up now.)

But the phone doesn't ring, the phone
doesn't ring; there are no e-mails
to download any more. I'm dusting

the last grains from my sandals;
I have nothing in my bag;
I'm preparing my c.v. In hallucinations

brought on by drought and prolonged
thirst in wildly unusual temperatures,
I'm starting to confuse images

of the Virgin Mary with Penélope Cruz.


## Titanium Man

He was titanium man, he was zinc man,
he was glue man and gesso man,
cheesecloth man, linen man,

rough cotton polyfilla man,
and his hands
were handmade papermakerman's hands.

Because this month, month one
in an estimated who knows how many months,
this month was white month.

White blooms
from the florist's and the hedgerows
arranged on the hearth:

hog peanut,
Dutchman's breeches,
cuckoo flower.

Collages from torn sheets
of inkjet printer paper,
every variety, three different gauges ...

But two hours twenty-seven minutes
going through the tracks
he'd got on his laptop

trying to find music
evoking the tones of snow
and he realised he might have gone

a shade too far. He collected
his thoughts and catalogued them
like butterflies. He was learning to paint

one colour at a time.


## All My Love

All this last weekend
I've re-lived the slow summer
we spent deconstructing
Smetana's

string quartets
using collage
and colour coding.
On the village

playing field this morning
green woodpeckers
were grazing –
that flash of childish colour

that red and yellow,
that move to a home key
against those predictable
jumbled greys.

# Percebes

Despite the Ventaxia,
which strains at the air, throbbing like a klaxon,
the whole house smells of the sea.
It is a fog coming ashore in the kitchen.

They're preparing a celebration dish,
a kind of barnacle. Which has a name all
of its own, but which looks like a fist
of witch's fingernails.

You tear away a finger,
peel it back, crack it
open, & there, like the untanned ring
beneath your real ring, is the pinky bit

of flesh you eat, for its mild briny
moistness. They tell you about the collectors
dangling in oilskins over slimy
rocks on the Galician, the Asturian shore.

You try to taste the danger they're
enjoying. You find it unexpectedly sweet.
You breathe the smell of the sea, its iodine air.
Their body language conveys how much of a treat

this is. And out of the sea-fog, the kitchen
sea-fog like the sea-fog in a children's story,
where it shapes knights in armour or wizened
old men or other kinds of sorcery,

a form solidifies; wipes her wet, black hair
from her eyes, gently drifts the beads
of water from her breasts, and stands tall there,
in the kitchen, her hips dangling seaweed.

# Late Bus

Supine under starlight,
Martin Mayer and me
and a girl from Willy Perks'

who was doing astronomy
for A-level (an option
our school didn't allow).

A winter night, frost
in the air like pollen,
the crystal heavens clear

as an illustration,
and she had a glossary at her
fingertips: celestial,

perihelion, syzygy...
We hung on her words
like bees hang on summer

and stared into the dark
spaces of the constellations,
seeing her there, of course,

light years over our heads.

# De Havilland Rapide

I was born in 1938, in disgrace,
in an aeroplane, a biplane,
a de Havilland Dragon Rapide,

shaking like a prototype, a fever,
a bicycle on the cobbles of Gold Hill,
Shaftesbury; an aeroplane, droning

over the Channel, the coast and a Picardy
manor house left derelict since the Great War;
and groaning like a woman in labour.

That's me, born on an aeroplane,
over France, in 1938. I have a photo
here, black and white, well, sepia,

of my loving mother;
and that sausage, that bundle,
that bolster in her arms,

that's me. 1943. Actually, I see,
it was an air balloon. I remember:
an air balloon floating over Buckinghamshire.

Or Oxfordshire. Southern England,
anyway. Or the Midlands. Whatever.
I remember my mother telling me,

years later, about wind direction,
and the way the trees at Blenheim
Palace are laid out to recreate

the military formation of the battle,
the battle of Blenheim. 1704.
1948. So that makes me 45 now.

45 years old. Can you credit it?
So, after all, it must have been –
what is it? – 1956. The Suez crisis.

And, come to think of it, it was.
As the doctor was slapping the bloody me
into life, into my very first breath,

like a butcher asserting the quality
of his raw material, well, just at that
very moment, that exact very moment,

that second, that instant, that stitch in time,
Bertolt Brecht, the wrestler,
the writer, the candlestick maker,

drew his very last breath somewhere
in communist Eastern Europe,
suggesting pretty definitively

that if Bertolt Breath had been
the Dalai Lama instead of a playwright,
stand-up comedian and part-time barber –

you should see his portfolio of styles –
no doubt several months later, or even
maybe years, having waited maybe

through lean decades in the meantime,
a gang of communists in big funny hats
and red badges would have knocked

on the door somewhere, maybe here,
to anoint me politely
in the name of the fatherland, the gun

and the Rolls Royce Silver Ghost.
Records in fact suggest Herr Brecht
finished his last act on August 14th,

nearly eight months later.
I might have got that wrong,
out of place, arse about face,

because
I always get Brecht mixed up with Donald
Campbell, January 4th

1967. Bloody air balloon.

# Saradha Soobrayen

SARADHA SOOBRAYEN was born in London in 1974. She received an Eric Gregory Award in 2004 and facilitates poetry workshops and professional development for writers across London. She is the Poetry Editor of *Chroma: A LGBT Literary Arts Journal* and has hosted *Chroma* events at literature festivals. Saradha has given readings of her work at the Royal Festival Hall, the Victoria and Albert Museum and the Essex Book Festival. Her prose has been published in *Kin: New Fiction by Black and Asian Women* (Serpents' Tail, 2003). Her poems have been included in: *Wasafiri, Poetry Review, This Little Stretch of Life* (Hearing Eye, 2006), *I am twenty people!* (Enitharmon, 2007), *New Writing 15* (Granta / The British Council, 2007) and the 2007 *Oxford Poets Anthology* (Carcanet Press).

# On the water meadows

I blame the twilight for coming too soon,
not allowing enough time for you
to drown without dying. And now
the water boatmen skate on the skin
of water, we should have practised
how to breathe. Instead we undressed
each other slowly: middle names, first
loves, spiders, toads and newts. Taking our
time to visit every corner, all the while
knowing we would soon run out of self.
I want to ignore the silver scar
on your left retina: the imprint of an iceberg.
Those places you were yearning for: Bermuda,
Pacific, Icelandic waters. Confident diver
that you are, land was never your best side.
What remains is the space around
your hands, their quietness, and at the tips
of fingers the faint hum of blue.

# Like cold air passing through lips

I shall think of you as my ventriloquist,
lying under the cedar trees. Your lips
unreadable, my mouth daydreaming:
journey, draining, geranium.
My head heavy more with rhymes than sleep,
resting on your arm, near the shadow's edge.
The fragrance of wood neither green
nor brown, but shallow blue.
Your compliments lodged in me
like harvest mice nesting under leaves,
foxgloves at our feet, the north winds singing.
My ear as dumb as corn and too far gone,
to catch your heart closing like a gate behind me.

## Questioning the invisible stitching

Don't make me reach for you
with the anxiety of a first-time traveller,
in the spirit of a truant, unable to love.
Now that the sparkle has gone, this poem remains
sleepily in my mind, breaking into snippets.
I'm lost in this twilight unlike you unwinding
our threads, mending holes in warm pockets of air
or magic. So much was up your sleeve: the birth of books,
musing on whether a rhyme equals hard work
and the art of disappearing. A sleight of hand and I am left
under a spell, with some minutes not yet uncoiled,
making you more precious. These hours are written
while the air is thick with thinking errors. A fleeting chill;
a moth dashes across my eyes, back and forth.

A moth dashes across my eyes back and forth
while the air is thick with thinking errors – a fleeting chill
making you more precious. These hours are written
under a spell, with some minutes not yet uncoiled,
and the art of disappearing; a sleight of hand. And I'm left
musing on whether a rhyme equals hard work
or magic? So much was up your sleeve: the birth of books,
our threads mending holes in warm pockets of air.
I'm lost in this twilight, unlike you, unwinding
sleepily in my mind, breaking into snippets.
Now that the sparkle has gone this poem remains
in the spirit of a truant. Unable to love,
with the anxiety of a first-time traveller,
don't make me reach for you.

# From the writing room

But why does she disappear for hours,
days, years without a blink, to her silver corners?
I arrive and leave and still catch her sighs
as she tidies her upright pencils, standing,
musing, while I rest, yet sinking a little
when I enquire about supper. Oh what misery,
the times waiting, meowing in vain.
And love, only the sound of it today.
A dish clinks on the tiles, the shoe brush
shunts backwards, a cushion sneezes under me.
This morning as I minced around Fitzroy Square
in between the chop-chopping of people
she became indistinct, blended, so not mine.
Moments were lost in the pigeons cooing.
A quickness surged through me and all the alleys
ever loved furred on my tongue and I was ready
to leap but I am held by the slant of her neck,
her reading mouth. The way her sounds
and words feed my stomach replacing gut
instinct with verse; tailbones with verbs.
Sometimes I offer to share my most precious
thoughts: truffles, treacle, tenderloin.
She listens, deeply unable to catch my drift.

# Stones from a Welsh pebble beach

She once made soup from stones: large flat greys
and yellow-veined white stones. She laid them out
on my writing desk and pointed out the red ore
hidden in the bluish blacks. She lined the pot,
made a mountain, ran cold water through the cracks
swirled salt with her fingers and watched the bubbles
blow up and burst. Cupping her hands around my ear,
she whispered: 'Come and taste, the sigh of seaweed,
the dull ache of wood breaking on the sand.'

# Xx

This time I have made you into the lower curve
of the letter 'S' and taken the top part for myself,
or if you prefer we could turn over on our sides
and both be touching the bottom line.
This is just word play; there is more to come:
sleeping in your half turns the sheets to silk.
I am dreaming this thought to myself. Here
and somewhere out there, you are just turning
a corner, if only I could head that way and leave
behind my slight temperature and pyjama's bottoms
and meet your highs and lows. The sky
is not ready nor the moon with its mystic
impulses. I am rather ordinary and not ready.
Desire has made us both uptight strokes
of the letter 'N' with only a diagonal line keeping
the peace. When I lean in, you barely give,
using the same amount of force by being still.
Sometime soon we shall topple over: left or right,
– your choice – and land soundly into the letter 'Z'.

---

# Lioness

Three square yards hold the silence of your roar,
what kind of beast wounds you, ignores your cries?
One stray kiss shames me, hardens my tongue, draws me
to your towering shoulders. Speak starry skies,
why is love not enough? Oh wild mother,
why hide your rumbling throat? Unclench your jaw,
soften your tongue, now lay down your head, daughter
of red earth, yellow grasses. The ground lies sore,
this gorge bleeds swollen, your eyes cry the shapes
of heavy moons. Your heart, dear Lioness, feels more
humane, pining for unbroken landscapes –
foothills, bare slopes, caverns moist at the core.
Within me are volcanoes rasping with spittle
and thunder so rude not even ash can settle.

# Marcus and me

Marcus and me like to wear
three jumpers to school.
The teacher tells me to say
the word 'warm' at least
seven times a day. But Marcus
says that warm is too small
a word, it moves away
too quickly like a mouse.

Marcus says that Anaemia
are little creatures, like lice.
He thinks he's caught them
by sucking the daisy foam
off my wallpaper.
Mum might have it too,
her pale face and kisses
taste of copper coins.

She doesn't mind Dad's
barking. Will it kill her?
Like her too-tight shoes or
an Asthma Attack? Marcus
sometimes hides outside
my parents' room. His ear
to the wall, his finger scraping
the paint off the radiator.

When Marcus and me have
an earache we go to my mum
and kneel like a donkey, my head
sideways on her lap, catching
the splashes one drop,
two drops. Mums rounds up
the wild hair from my ear but
her thumb can't shut out the thunder.

## My Little One          Mo Ti Bébé

| My Little One | Mo Ti Bébé |
|---|---|
| You jump right out too soon, | To fine sorti trop vite, tro petit |
| too small. You scream all times, | To crier tout le temps, |
| too much, too loud. | trop beaucoup, trop fort. |
| | |
| You cry near breast, near girl, | To pleuré prés cote mon sein, |
| | prés ma fille, |
| near boy. No time to cook, | prés mon garçon. Pas de temp |
| no time to clean. | pour cuire, pas de temp pour |
| | nettoye. |
| | |
| You twist, you turn, you clench, | To virer, tourner, to serre to |
| | poignet, |
| you kick, you push, you pull, | to donne coup pied, to pouser, |
| | to tire, |
| you fight your sleep. | to lagueure avek to sommeil. |
| | |
| You claw your eyes, you spit | To griffe to lizeaux, to crase |
| my milk. No time to sit, | mo dilait. Pas de temp pou asizer |
| no time to stand. | Pas de temp pour deporter. |
| My skin inside is swollen blue. | Mo lapeau endan fin devenir |
| | bleu. |
| | |
| Outside of me, outside of house, | En detoir moi, en detoir la caze, |
| | to sourir |
| you smile at birds, at trees, at | avec zoiseau, avec arbres, avec |
| clouds. | nuages. |
| Your body still as ginger root. | To le corp raid couma un razine |
| | zinzame. |
| | |
| I bind your hands with cotton | Mo attaché to lamain avec |
| strips, | cotton, |
| blanket wrap you straight and | mo envelop toi bien avec enn |
| neat, | molton |
| and leave the breeze to sway | et laisse la breeze prend to |
| your sleep. | sommeil. |

# My Conqueror

She circles me with her Portuguese compass
and settles just long enough to quench her thirst.
She discards my Arabian name *Dina Arobi*,
and calls me *Cerné*, from island of the swans.

With the hunger of a thousand Dutch sailors
and a tongue as rough as a sea biscuit she stakes
a longer claim and makes herself comfy,
bringing her own Javanese deer, pigs and chickens.

Defending her lust for breasts and thighs, she blames
the ship's rats for sucking the dodo from its shell.
Looking past my ebony limbs, she sees carved boxes
and *marron* hands at work stripping my forests.

She renames me in honour of Prince Maurice
of Nassau. A good choice, sure to scare off pirates
keen to catch a bite of river shrimp, flamed in rum.
Disheartened by cyclones and rat bites, she departs.

For eleven years, I belong to no one. I sleep
to the purring of turtledoves. Sheltered by a circle
of coral reef, my oval shape rises
from the coast up to the peaks of mountains.

A westerly wind carries her back. She unbuttons
her blue naval jacket slowly and takes me.
I am her *Île de France*, her *petit pain*.
She brings spaniels. She captures *marrons*

who are pinned down and flogged, each time they run.
She takes her fill in Port Louis, shipping casks
of pure sweetness to the tea-drinking ladies of Europe.
Young Baudelaire jumps ship on his way to India.

His step-father wants to cure him of 'literature'.
Once a poet makes his mark, no tide can wash away
his words: '*Au pays parfumé que le soleil caresse.*'
And what can I say, he was so delicious!

Sadly sweet Baudelaire soon finds himself
in such a profound melancholy,
after seeing a whipping in the main square,
after two weeks, he sails to France, leaving me

a sonnet. With the pride and jealousy of
the British Admiralty she punishes me
with her passion for corsets, sea-blockades
and endless petticoats wide as the Empire.

The oldest profession is alive and thrives
in my harbours; strumpets and exports, cross-
dressing captains and girls in white breeches.
Boys who like boys who like collars and chains.

She brings a pantomime cast of *malabars*
and *lascars* to my shores. Their passage back
to India guaranteed, if only they can read the scripts.
The cane breaks backs. Tamil, Urdu, Hindi, cling

to their skins like beads of sweat. Hundreds of tongues
parched like the mouths of sweethearts in an arranged
ceremony. She is kind and ruthless and insists
on the Queen's English. At night Creole verve slips in

and makes mischief. Each time she comes she pretends
it's the first time she has landed here, but she soon
becomes bored. Tired of flogging and kicking
the dogs. She doesn't know which uniform to wear.

'I'm no one and everyone,' she complains.
'And you have no more distinguishing marks
left to conquer.' She pulls down her Union
Jack; it falls like a sari, around her bare feet.

---

Marrons: *Creole name given to the slaves taken from Madagascar and trans-
ported convicts;* malabars *and* lascars: *Hindu and Muslim indentured labourers.
These names are disparaging terms in Mauritian Creole.*

**Carcanet Press publishes the following first collections by poets included in the *New Poetries* series**

Cliff Ashcroft *Faithful*

Caroline Bird *Looking Through Letterboxes*

Miles Champion *Compositional Bonbons Placate*

Sophie Hannah *The Hero and the Girl Next Door*

Adam Johnson *The Playground Bell*

James Keery *That Stranger, the Blues*

Patrick McGuinness *The Canals of Mars*

Patrick Mackie *Excerpts from the Memoirs of a Fool*

David Morley *Scientific Papers*

Sinéad Morrissey *There Was Fire In Vancouver*

Togara Muzanenhamo *Spirit Brides*

Jeremy Over *A Little Bit of Bread and No Cheese*

Karen Press *Home*

Justin Quinn *The O'o'a'a' Bird*

Adam Schwartzman *The Good Life, The Dirty Life*

James Sutherland-Smith *In the Country of Birds*

Matthew Welton *The Book of Matthew*

Jane Yeh *Marabou*

Visit **www.carcanet.co.uk** to browse a complete list of Carcanet titles, find out about forthcoming books and order books at discounted prices.

Email **info@carcanet.co.uk** to subscribe to the Carcanet e-letter for poetry news, events and a poem of the week.